ŚILPA-ŚĀSTRAṀ

ŚILPA-ŚĀSTRAṀ

WITH INTRODUCTION, NOTES AND ENGLISH TRANSLATION

BY

PROF. PHANINDRA NATH BOSE, M.A.

Editor :
Prof. Pushpendra Kumar

EASTERN BOOK LINKERS
DELHI : : (INDIA)

Publishers :
EASTERN BOOK LINKERS
5825, New Chandrawal,
Jawahar Nagar, Delhi-7
Ph. : 23850287, 30919869
e-mail : ebl@vsnl.net

First Edition : 2006

Price : 150.00

ISBN : 81-7854-085-1

ŚILPA-ŚĀSTRAM
Edited by : **Prof. Pushpendra Kumar**

Type Setting : Ajay Printing Works, Delhi
Printed at : R.K. Offset, Delhi

CONTENTS

Chapter

INTRODUCTION

The present work has a special merit of its own. This Śilpa-Śāstra with its Uriyā commentary is still consulted by the Śilpins of Orissa, where even now a large number of artists can be found. These artists possess numerous palm-leaf manuscripts, which deal mainly with the Śilpa principles. They consult those manuscripts in building their houses, images and temples. It is very unfortunate that these manuscripts donot contain Sanskrit ślokas in correct Sanskrit. In most of the cases, they have corrupted Sanskrit slokas though their Uriyā commentary conveys the true meaning. They use the corrupted Sanskrit ślokas and hand them down from father to the son. The descendants of the old artists can now be found in Puri, where there are 30 families, in Bhuvaneśvara only two families and so in Yajpura in Orissa. As these artists use the texts constantly, they donot like to part with their manuscripts, which they regard as their treasure.

It should, however, be mentioned that the name Śilpa-śastra applied to this book, is a misnomer. Instead of calling it Śilpa-Śāstra, it is better to call it Vāstū-Śāstra, because the book does not deal with images, but with the building of houses. The name Śilpa-śāstra has been taken here in a general sense and used to denote the science of building also. It, therefore, falls in the same category with the works like Vāstū-vidyā,

Manuṣyālaya-candrikā and other books. In the ordinary sense of the term, Śilpa-śāstra includes not only the science of sculpture, but also the sciences of architecture and painting. The present work falls, as we know from the contents of the book, under the science of architecture. Fortunately for us, we have in Sanskrit other works dealing with the science of architecture. One is *Vāstū Vidyā* edited by M.M.T. Ganapati Śāstrī from Travancore. It deals with the examination of the earth suitable for Vāstu land and also with house-building. Another work edited by the same scholar is *Manusyālaya-candrikā*, dealing with the same subject. The third work is *Mayamatam,* from the same editor, dealing with houses, palaces, villages and towns. It is considered as a very valuable work on the science of architecture.

Śilparatnam—is another valuable book, edited by the well-known scholar MM.T. Ganapati Śāstrī. The complete book is not yet out, but it promises to be an important work on Indian art and architecture. It may be divided into two parts, the first one containing 46 chapters dealing with architectural subjects and the second one of 35 chapters treating mainly of Indian iconography. Unfortunately, at present only the first part is published containing only one chapter on painting, while the remaining chapters deal with varied topics such as the characteristics of an *ācārya* and of a *Śilpin*, the laying out of villages, towns, houses, palaces, doors, steps, *toraṇa, maṇḍapa, nātya-maṇḍapa* and other allied subjects.

Another such book is *Bṛhat Saṁhitā* (cal, 1317 B.S.) by the sage Varāhamihira. Though it deals mainly with astronomy, yet in chapter 53, it deals with *Vāstu-vidyā* and in chapter 56 with *Prāsāda-lakṣaṇaṁ*.

There are some books, which have only a few chapters devoted to this topic of *Vāstu*. One such book is *Yukti-kalpa-taru*, edited by Pandit Iśvara chandra śāstri.[1] Only one chapter of this book, namely, chapter 23, deals with *Vāstu*.

Samarāṅgaṇa-Sūtradhāra—is an interesting book on Indian architecture, composed by the king Bhojadeva of Dhara. It has been edited by M.M.T. Ganapati Śāstri.[2] It tries to trace the origin of *Śilpaśāstra* and represents Viśvakarman as speaking about those subjects to his sons. The book covers a wide range from the laying out of villages, cities and forts to the making of several instruments (*Yantras*), such as elephant machine, *Vimāna* machine, door-keeper machine, soldier machine and others.

Viśvakarmaprakāśam—is an other interesting book on Indian architecture, and is ascribed to Viśvakarman.[3] It begins with the examination of the soil suitable for *Vāstu* land. It also deals with *Vāstu-vidyā* in general.

Some of the *Purāṇas* also deal with the topic of *Vāstu*. Of these mention should be made—

(i) of the *Matsya Purāṇam*, which has chapters 252-257 dealing with *Vāstu-vidyā*,

(ii) of the *Agnipurāṇam*, chapter 106 on *Nagarādi Vāstu*,

---

1. Included in the Calcutta Oriental Series in 1917.
2. Included in the Gaekwad's Oriental Series in 1924.
3. Veṅkaṭeśvara Press, Bombay, Saṁvat 1971.

(iii) of the *Garuḍapurāṇam* chapter 46 on *Vāstu-nirnaya,* and chapter 47 on *Prāsāda lakṣaṇam.*

(iv) and of the *Bhaviṣya Purāṇam.*

Vāstuprakaraṇam—is a Ms. in the Mss. Department of the Viśvabhāratī Library, bearing No. 1614. It is written on paper in Devanāgrī character. There are 29 leaves. The name of the copyist is not given, nor the date is noted. It deals with the topic of *vāstu* and mentions several experts in *Vāstu-vidyā* such as Gautama, Gārgya and Viśvakarman.

Our Indian tradition ascribes many *Śilpa* works to many celebrated authors, who are known as *Vāstu-śāstropadesakas* (or instructors in the science of *Vāstu*) and who are eighteen in number, according to the *Matsyapurāṇam.* They are : (1) Bhṛgu, (2) Atri, (3) Vasiṣṭha, (4) Viśvakarman, (5) Maya, (6) Nārada, (7) Nagnajita, (8) Viśālākśa, (9) Purandara, (10) Brahmā, (11) Kumāra, (12) Nandīśa, (13) Śaunaka, (14) Garga, (15) Vāsudeva, (16) Aniruddha, (17) Śukra and (18) Bṛhaspati.[1]

We are not in a position to ascertain the works written by these traditional writers. We, however, get a list of twenty-five traditional works on *Śilpa* in the

---

1. भृगुरत्रि वसिष्ठश्च विश्वकर्मा मयस्तथा।
नारदो नग्नजिच्चैव विशालाक्षः पुरन्दरः ।। 1 ।।
ब्रह्मा कुमारो नन्दीशः शौनको गर्ग एव च।
वासुदेवोऽनिरुद्धश्च तथा शुक्रो बृहस्पति ।। 2 ।।
अष्टादशैते विख्याता वास्तुशास्त्रोपदेशकाः।

Agnipurāṇam.[1] They are :—

(1) Pañca-rātra

(2) Sapta-rātra

(3) Haya-Śīrṣa-tantra

(4) Trailokya-mohana-tantra

(5) Vaibhava-tantra

(6) Pauṣkara-tantra

(7) Nāradīya-tantra

(8) Śāṇḍilya-tantra

(9) Vaiśvaka-tantra

(10) Śaunaka-tantra

(11) Jñāna-Sāgara-Vāsiṣṭha-tantra

(12) Prahlāda-tantra

(13) Gārgya-tantra

(14) Gālava-tantra

---

1. प्रोक्तानि पंचरात्राणि सप्तरात्राणि वै मया।। 1।।
व्यस्तानि मुनिभिर्लोके पंचविंशति संख्यया।
हयशीर्षे तन्त्रमाद्यं तन्त्रं त्रैलोक्यमोहनम्।। 2।।
वैभवं पौष्करं तन्त्रं प्रह्लादं गार्ग्यगालवम्।
नारदीयं च संप्रश्नं शांडिल्यं वैश्वकं तथा।। 3।।
सत्योक्तं शौनकं तन्त्रं वासिष्ठं ज्ञानसागरम्।
स्वायंभुवं कापिलं च तार्क्ष्यं नारायणीयकम्।। 4।।
आत्रेयं नारसिंहाख्यमानन्दाख्यं तथारुणम्।
बौधायनं तथार्षेंतु विश्वोक्तं तस्य सारतः।। 5।।

(Agnipurāṇam, ch. 39)

(15) Svāyambhuva-tantra

(16) Kapila-tantra

(17) Tārkṣya-tantra

(18) Nārāyaṇīya-tantra

(19) Ātreya-tantra

(20) Nārasiṁha-tantra

(21) Ānanda-tantra

(22) Aruṇa-tantra

(23) Baudhāyana-tantra

(24) Arṣa-tantra and

(25) Tantra spoken to Viśva.

It will be seen from the above list that some of the works are known after the names of their authors, who are known to us from the list of the Matsyapurāṇam. Thus from a comparison of the above two lists, we get the following names of *Śilpa* works and those of their authors :—

(i) Ātreya-tantra by Atri

(ii) Jñāna-Sāgara-Vāsiṣṭha-tantra by Vasiṣṭha

(iii) Nāradīya-tantra by Nārada

(iv) Śaunaka-tantra by Śaunaka

(v) Gārgya-tantra by Garga

(vi) Tantra spoken by Viśva(-Karman).

Unfortunately, these traditional works on *Śilpa* are not in existence at the present day. They, however, served as the source of inspiration to many later *Śilpa* writers, who mention some of these traditional writers. Thus, *Manuṣyālaya-candrikā* mentions some of the names of these instructors, such as, Viśvakarman, and Kumāra.[1] Again, Varāhamihira in his *Bṛhatsaṁhitā* speaks of Garga as an *ācārya* about the science of architecture.[2] Of other previous instructors, he mentions Maya (57, 8) Nagnajit and Vasiṣṭha (ch. 58).

An unpublished Ms. *Vāstu-prakaraṇaṁ*[3] calls Gautama, Garga and Viśvakarman 'experts in *Vāstu-vidyā*,' (*Vāstu-Vidyā-Viṣārada*) and holds that the work is only a compilation from the previous works.

Indian tradition, therefore, ascribes several books on *Śilpa* to different sages, who are now known to us more as law-givers than as writers on *Śilpa*.

I. Viśvakarman

Let us now proceed to gather together the accounts of these traditional *Śilpa* writers. Let us begin with *Viśvakarman,* the most well-known figure in the whole of the Indian *Śilpa* literature. As he himself was an expert *Śilpin,* his name occurs frequently in the Paurāṇic literature. We must be careful in distinguishing *Viśvakarman,* the writer of the *Śilpa* texts from the Viśvakarman of popular myth. In the Brāhmaṇas, Viśvakarman is the same as the creator Prajāpatī.[4] This idea of the Creator is perhaps responsible for making Viśvakarman, the creator of material things. We have no doubt that there existed before the Gupta period of

1. ch. I. S. 8.
2. ch. 56, 5.31
3. Now in Viśvabhāratī Library.
4. Ved. myth. pp. 117-18.

Śilpa texts, Viśvakarman by name. His theory of *Śilpa* might have been very popular. So we find numerous stories current about him in Indian literature. Even at the present day, Viśvakarman is worshipped by Indian artisans on the ocasion of *Viśvakarma Pūjā*. His image is described by Hemādrī as follows :—

"*Viśvakarmā tu kartavyaḥ sura-rūpadharaḥ Saṁdaṁsapānir dvibhujas tejomūrti-dharo mahān.*"[1]

According to the *Matsya-purāṇam*, Viśvakarman was the son of Prabhasa. He was a *Prajāpati* (Patriarch), as well as a *Śilpin*. As a *Śilpin*, he was expert in the construction of palaces, houses gardens, images, ornaments, tanks and wells.[2]

The *Agnipurāṇam* calls Viśvakarman the creator of thousand *Śilpas* (crafts), with the help of which men earn their living.[3] The *Garuḍapurāṇam* also speaks of Viśvakarman as the famous *Śīlpin* of the gods.[4] From the *Mahābhārata*, we learn that Prabhāsa was the *father* of Viśvakarman and his mother was the sister of Bṛhaspatī. As in the *Agnipurāṇam* here also he was called the creator of thousand *Śilpas*, which were used by men as the means of their livlihood.[5]

---

1. Hemādrī-Vratakhaṇḍa, ch. 1. p. 104.
2. Matsyapurāṇam, ch. 5, s. 27-28.
3. कर्त्ता शिल्पसहस्राणां त्रिदशानां च वर्द्धकिः।
   मनुष्याश्चोपजीवन्ति शिल्पं वै भूषणादिकम्।।
   (Agnipurāṇam, ch. 18, s. 40-41)
4. Garuḍapurāṇam, ch. 6.5.36.
5. MBH. Ādiparvan, s. 2590-2593.

Mānasāra holds that of the four architects created from the four faces of Brahmā, the creator of the universe, the first was Viśvakarman.[1]

As the architect of the gods, Viśvakarman was engaged in building palaces for the divine beings. In Bharata's *Nāṭyaśāstram* we find Brahmā asking Viśvakarman to build a theatre hall. In a short time, the divine architect was able to construct an auspicious house, suitable for the theatrical purposes.[2]

In the *Rāmāyaṇa,* we find Viśvakarman building the city of *Laṅkā* for the dwelling of the Rākṣasas.[3] He also constructed palaces for the sage Agastya,[4] for Sūrya[5] and for Kubera.[6] It was he who had constructed the divine chariot (*Puṣpaka-ratha*) for the god Brahmā.[7]

In the *Skandapurāṇam* (māheśvarakhaṇḍe-kedārakhandam) Viśvakarman is described as building a meeting place, at the request of Himālaya. Not only did he construct a charming meeting-place, but adorned it with many figures of horses, peacocks and deer. He

---

1. Dr. P. K. Acharya—A Summary of the Manasara, p. 2.
2. ततस्तु विश्वकर्माणमाह ब्रह्मा प्रयत्नतः।
   कुरु लक्षणसम्पन्नं नाट्यवेश्म महामते।।
   ततोऽचिरेण कालेन विश्वकर्मा शुभं महत्।
   सर्वलक्षणसम्पन्नं कृत्वा नाट्यगृहं तु सः।।
   (Nāṭyaśāstram, ch. 1. s. 45-46)
3. Uttarakāṇḍam, ch. 3, s. 26.
4. Kiṣkindhākāṇḍam, ch. 41, s. 35.
5. Ibid., ch. 42, s. 44.
6. Ibid., ch. 43, s. 21.
7. Sundarakāṇḍam, ch. 9, s. 11.

also put there the beautiful images of various gods. In *Śrīmad Bhāgavatam* we read that Viśakarman also built a charming palace for Śrī Kṛṣṇa.[1]

Thus Viśvakarman appears not as much as a writer of *Śilpa* canons in the Paurāṇic and classical literature, but as an expert *Śilpin.* As such, he is rightly called by *Vāstu-vidyā* "the god of *Śilpins.*" A few *Śilpa* books, however, has been ascribed to him.

He is said to be the author of *Viṣvakarma-prakāśa,* of which two editions have been published : one from Benares in lithoprint in 1941 Saṁvat, the other one from Bombay (Veṅkaṭeśvara Press) in 1971 Saṁvat. At the end of the book, he is described as *mahāmā,* possessed of all good qualities and proficient in all the *Śāstras.* He is said to be the *sūtradhāra* of all gods. He wrote this *śāstra* for good of the men of this world.

Rām Rāz has utilised a few detached chapters of a *Śilpa* work called *Viśvacarmīya* for his *Essay.*[2] Dr. Rajendra Lal Mitra also spoke of three *Śilpa* Mss. ascribed to Viśvakarman :—

(i) *Viśvacarmīya* Ms. from Tanjore,

(ii) *Viśvakarmaprakāśa* from the library of Rājā Rādhā Kānta Deva.

(iii) *Aparājitā-pṛccā* (narrated by Viśvakarman) from the library of Asiatic Society of Bengal.[3]

1. Śrimad Bhāgavatam, X, ch. 59, s. 50-53
2. Essay on Hindu Architecture, p. 3.
3. R.L. Mitra—Indo-Āryans, Vol. 1, pp. 39-40.

The Oriental Ms. Library, Madras also has one Ms. named *Viśvakarmīyam Śīlpaśāstram.*

As to the age when Viśvakarman flourished, it may be mentioned that Varāhamihira in his *Bṛhatsaṁhitā* in the chapter on *Prāsāda-lakṣaṇam* quotes the opinion of Viśvakarman.[1]

सार्द्धं हस्तत्रयं चैव कथितं विश्वकर्मणा।।

We know with certainty, according to Dr. H. Kern that the most flourishing period of the life of Varāhamihira falls in the first half of sixth century of the Christian Era. If Varāhamitira flourished in the sixth century A.D. Viśvakarman must have flourished before the sixth century of the Christian Era. We, cannot, however, definitely settle the period when he flourished.

II- Maya

As Viśvakarman was the architect of gods, so *Maya* was the architect of the *asuras.* In the *Mahābhārata,* we find him building the assembly hall for the king Yudhiṣṭ hira. He takes pride, in calling himself a Viśvakarman of the *dānavas* and a great poet.[2] He also built three cities for the *dānavas.*[3] Maya was also called a *mahāsura* and Viśvakarman and was respected by the *daityas* and *dānavas.*

The *Matsyapurāṇam* calls Maya an instructor in

---

1. Bṛhatsaṁhitā, ch. 56, s. 29.
2. MBH. Sabhā Parvan, s. 5, अहं हि विश्वकर्मा वै दानवानां महाकविः।।
3. MBH, VIII. 33, 1406.

Vāstuśāstra. According to *Mānasara,* Maya was one of the four architects created from the four faces of Brahma.[1] In *Bṛhatsaṁhitā, Varāhamihira* quotes the opinion of Maya about palaces.[2] In the next chapter, he summarises the views of Maya regarding *Vajra-lepa.*[3]

These references to Maya and his opinion in Varāhamihira's work, prove the existence of Maya's work on *Śilpa* at the time of Varāhamihira (6th century A.D.).

At present some *Silpa* works are attributed to Maya. M.M.T. Ganapati Śāstrī has brought out an edition of *Mayamatam,* which is ascribed to *Mayamuni.* In *Mayamatam,* Muni Maya has been spoken of as wise and the originator of all *Vāstu-lakṣaṇa.*[4] Maya collected all that. had been uttered by Brahmā and other gods and sages. So he also based his work on the utterances of his predecessors.[5] *Mayamatam* deals chiefly with the construction of different styles of houses. The following works are also ascribed to Maya :—

(i) Māyamata-vāstu-śāstra (Madras Oriental Ms. Library, No. 13034-13039)

(ii) Maya-Vāstu (in Telegu character, Madras, 1916)

---

1. Dr. P. K. Acharya—A Summary of the Mānasara, p. 2.
2. Bṛhatsaṁhitā, ch. 56, s. 9, भूमिकांगुलमानेन मयसाष्टोत्तरं शतम्।।
3. Ibid., ch. 57, s. 8. मयकथि तो योगोऽयं वियोज्भवज्रसंघातः।।
4. Mayamatam, ch. 1, s. 2. प्राज्ञो मुनिर्मयः कर्त्ता सर्वेषां वास्तुलक्षणम्।।
5. Ibid., ch. 1, s. 12

(iii) Maya-Vāstu-śāstra (Madras, 1917)

(iv) Maya-Śilpaśāstra (in Tamil).[1]

III. Nagnajit

Nagnajit is mentioned in the *Matsyapurāṇam* as one of the eighteen instructors in the science of *Vāstu*. Varāhamihira quotes him as an older authority and calls his system *Draviḍa*.[2] We may, therefore assume that Nagnajit belonged to Southern India. In older literature, we read of a king Nagnajit, who is different from the *Śilpin* Nagnajit.

Nagnajit is also said to be the author of *Citra-lakṣaṇam;* whose Tibetan version exists even at the present day, though the original Sanskrit version is lost to us. In 1913 Berthold Laufer translated this book from Tibetan into German in the *Document der Indischen Kunst* Series. At the end of the first two chapters of *Citra-lakṣaṇam,* Nagnajit is mentioned as its author. A story as to the origin of *citra-vidyā* (the science of painting) is given in this book. The story runs thus : Formerly, during the reign of a virtuous king named Bhayajit, there was peace and prosperity in his kingdom. Once a Brahmin came to him crying : "Oh king, there is certainly sin in your kingdom, or why my young son would die untimely. Please get my son back from the other world." The king, accordingly, demanded the return of the Brahmin son from *Yama,* on whose refusal a fight began. Yama was defeated.

1. Translated into English in Indian Antiquary, vol. V, 1876, pp. 230-37, 293-97.
2. Bṛhatsaṁhitā, ch. 58.

Then came Brahmā, who told the king! "Life and death follow *karma.* Yama has nothing to do with them. Draw a picture of the Brahmin son and I shall give back life to him.." The king did so. Brahmā put life to that picture and told the king : "As you have conquered the *nagna-pretas* (naked ghosts) you will be hence-forth known as *Nagnajit.* You could draw this picture of the Brahmin son only through my grace. This is the first picture in this world. You go to the divine *Śilpin* Viśvakarman, who would teach you every thing regarding *citra-vidyā.*"[1]

IV. Vasiṣṭha

Vasiṣṭha is a well-known sage, born of the *Prāṇa* of Brahmā. Arundhati was his wife and the seven sages (*saptarṣī*) were his sons. He is one of the eighteen instructors in the science of *Vāstu* mentioned by *Matsyapurāṇam.* The *Agnipurāṇam* calls him the author of a *Śilpa* text, namely, *Jñāna-Sāgara-Vasiṣṭha, Tantra.* Varāhamihira also quotes him as an authority in his book *Bṛhat-Saṁhitā* in the chapter on *Pratimā-lakṣ aṇaṁ.*[2] We can, therefore, place him before the sixth century of the Christian Era.

V. Atri

Another famous law-giver, who appears also as a writer of *Śilpa* texts is —*Atri,* who is included in the group of *Saptarṣī* sages. He was born of the eye of Brahmā. The Matsyapurāṇam calls him an instructor

1. B. Laufer-Das Citralakṣaṇa (1913).
2. Bṛhatsaṁhita, ch. 58, s. 8.

in *Vāstu-śāstra,* while the Agnipurāṇam ascribes to him a *Śilpa* text, named *Ātreya-Tantra.*

VI. Nārada

Nārada though a divine sage (*devarṣī*), was born of a śūdra mother and a Brahmin father. According to *Mānasara,*[1] he is one of the sages from whom the *Vāstu-Śāstra* has come down to us. Besides, being an instructor in the *Vāstu-Śāstra,* he is known as the author of *Nāradīya-Tantra,* according to the *Agnipurāṇam.*

VII. Garga

Garga, the son of Brahmā and a well known sage, was the author of *Gārga-Tantra* according to the *Agni-purāṇam.* Not only *Matsyapurāṇam* calls him an instructor in *Vāstu-Śāstra,* but Varahammira also quotes him as an authority on the construction of palaces. Garga, therefore, should be placed before the sixth century A.D.

VIII. Kumāra

The *Matsyapurāṇam* holds *Kumāra* as a sage, competent to instruct in the science of *Vāstu, A Śilpa* work—*manuṣyālayacandrikā*[2] mentions *Kumārāgama,* which might be taken as a *Silpa* work written by the sage Kumāra. Another work *Śilpa-ratnam*[3] is ascribed to Śrī Kumāra, who is evidently a quite different man flourishing in Kerala in the latter part of the 16th century A.D.

IX. Śaunaka

Śaunaka, a sage, was responsible, according to

---

1. See—P. K. Acharya's A Summary of Mānasara.
2. Edited by M.M. T. Ganpati Śāstri and published by the Travancore Government.
3. Edited by MM. T. Ganpati Sastri.

the *Agnipurāṇam,* for a *Śilpa* work called *Śaunaka Tantra.* He is another *Vāstuśāstropadeśaka,* according to the *Matsyapuranam.*

X. Viśālākṣa

Viśālākṣa is a sage well-known in *rājanīti* literature. He is regarded as an authority on politics even by Kauṭilya, who quotes his opinion in his *Arthaśāstra.*[1] He is also referred to by Somadeva, a Jain writer in his *Yaśastilaka-campu* as a writer of a *Nītiśāstra.*[2] He is regarded by *Matsyapurāṇam* an instructor in the science of *Vāstu.*

XI. Śukra

Śukra is known as the *guru* of the *daityas,* as such he is competent to instruct in various branches of learning. He is liberally quoted by Somadeva in his *Nītivākyāmṛtam* as an authority in *Nītiśāstra.* The same author in his *Yaśāstilakacampū* regards him as a famous writer of *Nītiśāstra.* In *Śukranīti,* which is ascribed to the sage Śukra, we find chapters dealing with the construction of houses, palaces and images.[3] He is also an instructor in the science of *Vāstu.*

XII. Bṛhaspatī

Bṛhaspatī, the *guru* of the gods, in well-versed in all branches of science. *Mānasara* calls him one of the sages from whom *Vāstuśāstra* has come down to us. He is another instructor in the science of *Vāstu.*

---

1. Kauṭilya's Arthaśāstra, p. 13.
2. Yaśastilakacampū, p. 236.
3. Translated by B. K. Sarkar in Sacred Books of the Hindus Series.

XIII. Prahlāda

The *Agnipurāṇam* mentions a work on *Śilpa, Prahlāda Tantra* by name. As the name suggests the writer of this text was *Prahlāda*. In *Citra-lakṣaṇam,* we hear of the School of Prahlāda mentioned along with that of Viśvakarman.

The materials of our disposal are so meagre, that it is not possible for as to picture a comprehensive biography of each of the writers of *Śilpaśāstra.*

WRITERS ON ŚILPA

In the present age, it was reserved for Rām Rāz, a Judge and magistrate of Bangalore, to draw the attention of Indologists to the unexplored field of *Śilpaśāstra.* His *Essay on the architecture of the Hindus*[1] marked 'an epoch not only in the history of science, but also in that of the Hindus themselves.' As a pioneer, Rām Rāz encountered tremendous difficulties by reason of the absence of literature on the subject, as well as the lack of sympathy and help from the *Śilpin.* He procured portions of *Mānasāra, Mayamata, Kasyapa* and *Vayghansa* and a few detached chapters of (1) *Sacaladhicara,* (2) *Viśvaśarmīya,* (3) *Sanatkumāra,* (4) *Sāraswatyam,* (5) *Pañcarātram.* In his *Essay,* he gave a detailed account of *Mānasara* along with the first three works.

He was followed by Dr. Rajendra Lal Mitra, who in his *Antiquities of Orissa* dealt with the whole subject of architecture. He spoke of four Mss. not utilised by Rām Rāz. They are :—

1. Published in 1834 for Oriental Translation Fund of Great Britain and Ireland.

(i) *Mānasara* in the library of Asiatic Society of Bengal,

(ii) *Viśvakarmīya* from Tanjore,

(iii) *Viśvakarmaprakāśa* in the library of Rāja Rādhākānta Deva,

(iv) *Aparājita-pṛcċha* in the library of Asiatic Society of Bengal.[1]

In 1908 Dr. A. Coomaraswamy in his *Mediaeval Sinhaleṣe Art* treated of the history of art in Ċeylon with special reference to Indian art. He gathered together references to *Visvakarman* in the Sinhalese chronicle *Mahā Vamsa* and other Ceylonese literature.[2] In chapter IV, he spoke of a Sinhalese work *Rupāvalīya,* which is part of the artistic cannon of Sinhalese painters. The book is ascribed to Indian origin and is mainly relied on by Kandyan painters of the best sort. In chapter V, he described another Sinhalese work on art named *Mahamataya,* which is said to have been translated from Sanskrit in A.D. 1837. Lastly, in chapter VIII, he gave a translation of another work on art, Sāriputra, which deals with the dimensions of images in general and of Buddha in particular.

In 1913 Berthoḷd Laufer translated *Citra-lakṣaṇam* from Tibetan into German. He published the Tibetan text along with the German translation of the same. The work is attributed to *Nagnajit,* from whose name,

---

1. Indo-Aryans, Vol I, pp. 39-40.
2. Mediaeval Sinhalese Art, pp. 78-79.

Laufer infers that the book is of Jaina origin, though included in the Buddhiust Encyclopaedia.

In 1914 T.A. Gopinatha Rao, the Superintendent of Archaeology, Travancore State, brought out his *Element of Hindu Iconography,*[1] in which he used *Rūpa-maṇḍana* and eight other works on Śaivāgama giving minute descriptions of Vaiṣṇava and Śaiva images.

Then followed Mr. O. C. Ganguly with his *South Indian Bronzes,*[2] which gives a historical survey of South Indian Sculpture with iconographical notes based on original sources. In this Volume Mr. Ganguly used three original Sanskrit manuscripts dealing with the sculptor's canons, namely, *Kāśyapīya, Agastiya* and *Brāhmīya.*

In 1918 Dr. Prasanna Kumar Acharya brought out *A Summary of the Mānasāra : A Treatise on Architecture and Cognate object.*[3] We have in this book a summary of the *Mānasāra,* which he proposed to edit critically on the basis of the available manuscripts, specially that of India office. "The object of this summary of *Mānasāra*", says Dr. Acharya, "is nothing more than to introduce the various topics in brief . . . . It might at the same time throw a little light, for the first time, upon one of the most useful and hitherto unknown branches of scientific studies." The *Mānasāra* deals not only with *Vāstu*, but also with the laying out of *Nagara,* fort, *Vimāna, Gopura, Maṇḍapa,* royal

1. Madras, 1914.
2. Published by the Indian Society of Oriental Art, Calcutta, 1915.
3. Leiden, 1918.

palace, thrones, ornaments and images of various gods and goddesses.

Dr. Abanindra Nath Tagore, who stands out pre-eminently as the leader of the Indian art-revival, wrote several books on Indian art. Of these we may mention his *Sadaṅga* and *Anatomy of the Hindu Art,* which are published by the Indian Society of Oriental Art of Calcutta. In 1921, Andre Karples translated into French *Art et Anatomie Hindous*[1] Karples also translated Dr. Tagore's book *L' Alpana.*

Mr. A.K. Maitra of the Varendra Research Society contributed several articles on *Śilpa* in the *Rūpam,* in which appeared his article, on *Aims and methods of Painting in ancient India.*[2] From Rajshahi, Pandit Girish Chandra Vedānta-tīrtha published a valuable book in Bengali called *Pracīna Śilpaparicaya,*[3] in which he collected all the available materials on vaious *Śilpas,* such as painting image-making and various kinds of ornaments.

Last, though not the least, comes the well-known scholar of Travancore, MM. T. Ganapati Śāstri, who has rendered yeomen service to the cause of Sanskrit literature in general and *Śilpaśāstra* in particular. He has edited *Vāstuvidyā* (in 1913), *Manuṣyālayachandrikā* (in 1917), *Mayamatam* (in 1919) and *Śilparatnam,* (in 1922)..

---

1. Paris, 1912.
2. Rupam, Jan-June, 1923.
3. Calcutta, 1923, B.S.

MEANING OF ŚILPA, VĀSTU AND KALĀ

So long we are using the words *Śilpa* and *Vāstu* rather loosely. There is also a general tendency of confusing these two terms. Another term, which is generally used as synonymous, is *Kalā*. It is necessary to note the difference of these terms : *Śilpa, Vāstu* and *Kalā*.

Mr A. K. Maitra holds that *Śilpaśāstra* is included in *Vāstuvidyā*. He remarks : "The *Śilpaśāstram* was virtually a competent part of the *Vāstuśāstram*, the science of architecture."[1] Dr. P.K. Acharya in his article on the *Training of architects in ancient India*[2] also expressed the same view. It seems to us that *Śilpaśāstra* is a general term. It includes all fine arts, while *Vāstuśāstra* includes only the science of architecture. In *Vāstuśāstra* are enumerated the qualifications of *Śilpins*, in which category the writer includes an architect (*Sthapati*), a carpenter *(sūtra-grāhī)*, a sculptor (*tākṣaka*) and a moulder (*mṛtkarmajña*).[3] In the *Brahmavaivartapurāṇam* (*Brahmakhaṇḍa*, ch. 10), we find that the sons of Viśvakarman are called *Śilpakārinaḥ*. They are nine in number, namely *Mālākāra* (a garland-maker), *Karmakāra* (a blacksmith), *Śaṅkhakāra* (a conch-maker), *Kabindaka* (a weaver), *Kumbhakāra* (a potter) *Kaṁsakāra* (a maker of bell-metal), *Sūtradhāra* (a carpenter), *Citrakāra* (a painter), and *Svarṇakāra* (a goldsmith). Here we find *Śilpa* used in a general sense to include various arts and crafts.

---

1. Rūpam, p. 19, 1923.
2. Rūpam, Oct., 1922.
3. Vāstuvidyā, ch. 1.

The earliest mention we get of the term *Śilpa* is in the *Kauṣītaki Brāhmaṇa*[1] where *Śilpa* is taken as equivalent to "art" and is said to be of three kinds, *nṛtya* (dance), *gīta* (song) and *Vādita* (instrumental music). In the *Mahābhārata,* we find mention of a thousand *Śilpas,* of which Viśvakarman was the creator and which were used by men as the means of their livilihood.[2] In the classical literature *Śilpa* has been used in a general sense to include all kinds of art.

The term *Kalā* has been used in the Ṛg Veda to denote a fractional part.[3] Gradually it came to mean branches of art. Both the terms *Śilpa,* and *Kalā* were used by our older writers in a loose sense so it is very difficult to draw a line of demarcation between the two, as in the *Rāmāyaṇa :*

नानाशिल्पकलाज्ञश्च भवेरपि परन्तप ।[4]

Here *Śilpa* may be taken as to mean "arts" and *Kalā* "Sciences".

In the Pāli literature, the word *Śilpa* (*Sippa*) was rather used to mean the sciences. In *Jātaka* stories, we hear of *Sabbasippanī*[5] to mean all the sciences, which according to Fick,[6] include not only the three Vedas, but also the eighteen branches of science.

In *Lalitavistara,* we find mention of *Karma-Kalās*[1] and sixty-four *Kāma-kalās.*[2] In *Kalpa-Sūtra,* we get

1. XXIX, 5.
2. Adiparvan, s. 2500-2503.
3. VIII, 47, 17.
4. Vol. I, pp. 301-5.
5. I, 463, II, 53, III 219.
6. Social Organisation etc. p. 202.

seventy-two *kalās.*[3] In Jaina Sūtras, we read that Samudrapāla studied seventy-two *kalās* (arts).[4] They are also refered to by Vātsyāyana in his *Kāmasūtra*[5] and by many later writers.

It is difficult to settle the number of *Kalās.* Though the later writers fixed the number at sixty-four, there is no uniformity of opinion among earlier writers. Both Vātsyāyana and *Śṛmad Bhāgavata* put the number at sixty-four, the Jain books take seventy-two, *Lalitavistara* sixty-four, while Yaśodhara in his commentary of the *Kāma-Sūtra* carries the number to 512.

Thus we find that almost every subject under the sun has been grouped under the term *kalā.* Our Indian writer rather used both the terms *Śilpa* and *Kalā* loosely. In the Vedic literature, *Śilpa* is said to be of three kinds : *nṛtya* (dance), *gīta* (song) and *Vādita* (instrumental music). Even these three branches of knowledge are enumerated in Vātsyāyana's *Kāmasūtra* under the head *Kalās; gītam* singing), *vādyam* (instrumental music), and *nṛtyam* (dancing).

In the inscriptions, the engraver is also known as the *Śilpin.* Thus, we find that the Dhāra Praśasti of Arjunavarman was engraved by the *Śilpin* (artist) Rāmadeva, the son of the excellent sculptor *(rūpakāra)*

---

1. p. 179.
2. p. 417
3. p. 74.
4. Uttarādhyayana, Jaina Sūtras, S.B.E. vol. 45, p. 108.
5. p. 42, 95.

Sīhāka.[1] Again, the Sāranath inscription of Kumāra Devī was engraved by the *Śilpin* Vāmana.[2]

Bharata tries to set the controversy at rest when he says :—

वात्स्यायनोक्तनृत्यगीतवाद्यादिश्चतुपष्ठिः बाह्यक्रियाः तथा आलिंगनचुम्बनादि श्चतुषष्ठिः अभ्यन्तरक्रियाः कलाः। आदिना स्वर्णकारादिकारुकर्मव्रहः। एततृसर्वं शिल्पं कथ्यते। इति तट्टीकायां भरतः।

According to Bharata, therefore, not only the sixty-four external actions such as *nṛtya* (dancing), *gīta* (singing), *vādya* (instrumental music) and others, which are spoken of by Vātsyāyana, but also the sixty-four internal actions, such as embracing and kissing—are known by the name *Kalā.* All this as well as the work of goldsmith and others, are known as *Śilpa.*

Thus, we may conclude that *Śilpa* is a general term, under which are included *Kalās.* At different times, the *Kalās* have been differently enumerated by different authors and they have come to include all sorts of five. *Śilpa* may be said to mean all fine arts and crafts.

There was a tendency in ancient India not to encourage the culture of such fine arts as dancing and singing. In the *Institute of Manu,* we read that practising the arts of dancing and singing was regarded as an offence.[3] Manu also lays down that an actor or singer should be avoided.[1] Manu even goes so far as to hold that dancers and singers should be banished from the

1. Epigraphia Indica, VIII, p. 98.
2. Ibid., IX, p. 326.
3. S.B.E., vol. 25 (XI, 66, p. 443).

town.[2] These seem to point to the fact that the arts of dancing and singing were not greatly encouraged at least in the days of Manu.

Are the fine arts, then, derived from the non-Aryan group? It is difficult to answer this question definitely. We know that the term *Kalā,* has been derived from the Draviḍian root *Kal,* to learn. Perhaps the *Kalās* were borrowed from the Draviḍians, for that reason, those people, who specialised in the fine arts and crafts were not highly regarded in the society. They were banished from the town or were looked upon as offenders.

In Pāli literature, we donot find any systematic work about the construction of buildings. In Bhikṣu Pratimòkṣa, we get references to the building of cottages. Ālabira bhikṣus built some cottages for their own use. They had begged the materials from the householders, who became quite disgusted with their demands. So, Lord Buddha made the following rule : If a Bhakṣu wants to build a cottage for his own use after begging for materials from others, that cottage must be built according to the rule, namely, 12 Vitasti (Sugata-Vitasti) in length and 7 Vitasti in breadth. Other bhikṣus must be brought in to select the *Vāstu,* which should have so much space all around that a cart drawn by the bullocks might pass round it. If a bhikṣu breaks this rule, he would be sent away from the order.

Thus, according to the lord Buddha, the cottage for the monks would be 12 Vitasti in length and 7 Vitasti

1. S.B.E., Vol. 25`, III, 155.
2. Ibid., 225. In the Vinaya also Buddhist monks are prohibited from taking part in songs and dances.

in breadth. Now, what is this Vitasti? Buddhaghoṣa says that it is equal to the three Vitastis of the present generation. The monks of Ceylon take the foot print of Lord Buddha on Adam's peak as a Vitasti. It is 4 hands in length. According to Buddhaghoṣa the length of the cottage would be 18 cubits and breadth 10½ cubits. But according to the Sinhalese monks, it would be 48 hands long and 28 hands broad. In Buddhist books we hear of three kinds of cottages :

(1) उल्लिता (उल्लिप्ता), whose inside has been covered with mud or *cūnam.*

(2) अवल्लित्ता (अवलिप्ता) whose outside has been covered with mud.

(3) उल्लित्तावल्लित्ता (उल्लिप्तावल्लिप्ता) whose both sides have been covered with mud.

A bigger house, a vihāra may be constructed by a *bhikṣu,* if there is a donor and if it is meant for the bhikṣu himself. Its Vāstu must be specified by other monks and there must be sufficient space all round for a bullock-cart to pass. Such a Vihāra is called महल्लक।

From Cullavagga (6,I.1-2) we know of the origin of Vihāra. At first the monks used to live under trees and in mountain caves. Seeing this a Śreṣṭhin of Rājagṛha expressed his desire to Lord Buddha of building Vihāras for the use of monks. Hearing the proposal, Buddha sanctioned five kinds of abodes for monks, namely :

(1) विहार

(2) आढ्ययोग

(3) प्रासाद

(4) हर्म्य

(5) गुहा।

It seems that once there existed a vast mass of literature of Śilpaśāstra in India. It may be that this branch of learning remained confined to a section of artists, who made śilpa their profession. In the beginning, these śilpins used to get a sound training not only in their śilpas, but also received general education. According to the *Vāstuvidyā,* the architect must be expert in all śāstras, must not be crippled, must be kind, and virtuous, knowing mathematics, Purāṇas, the art of painting, the geography of all countries and Vāstu-vidyā (ch. 1, s. 12-15). As the Śilpins were men of education and culture, it was not difficult for them to understand the Śilpa texts. Gradually, however, they began to neglect general education, to which they gave a very unimportant place in their lives. The natural result of this lack of education was that they could but little understand the Sanskrit Śilpa texts. They had, however, one advantage. As the profession had become hereditary, they could get the benefit of practical training from their fathers. So the use of texts began to be dispensed with and the texts began to be regarded as sacred and often worshipped as such by the śilpins. When these sacred texts began to be worn out and the necessity arose of copying them, the texts began to change at the hands of the illiterate copyists. In many cases those texts became so corrupted that it is next to impossible to restore the original version. Many manuscripts can still be found with the artists in Orissa, but they are so scrapulous about those manuscripts that they do not allow any curious eye to watch over them. They often keep them in wooden chests, where the worms play havoc and destroy the mss. so carefully kept. Thus many mss. have perished and those which escape the destruction from fire and worms, are now in a corrupted form. In many cases, jt requires herculean patience to restore the original form. I am thankful to Ravi Malhotra to include this work in their publication.

P. Kumar

Delhi
2 October, 2005

PREFACE TO THE PRESENT TEXT

All the texts of Śīlpaśāstra published so far belong mainly to Southern India. The present work belongs to Orissa and as such is one of the Śilpaśāstra of Northern India. It is based on the following materials :—

(1) Ms.A.—is called *Śilpa sadajaya*-

It begans thus :

श्री गणसाए नमः। अथ सिल्प लिक्षते।
ब्रह्मक्षेत्रीं वस शुद्रं शुक्लारक्तापिताय।
कृष्णवर्ण च क्रमेणा अतैव वास्तुलक्षण।।

It ends thus :

इति शिल्पिसदाजये संपूर्ण।
श्रीशुभमस्तु श्रीश्रीशुभमस्तु। श्रीश्रीसर्वशुभमस्तु।
ए शिल्पियुथि वन्तलि गाँर करुणि माहाराणापुत्र नीलकण्ठ महाराणार।

This Ms. belongs to Nīlkaṇṭha Mahārāṇā, son of Karuṇi Māhārāṇā of the village of Bantali (in Orissa). The owner of the Ms. is still living and is a *Śilpin* by profession. We are using the copy prepared from his ms, by my friend Sri Nirmal Kumar Bose. The name of the author does not appear in the body of the text, but it is almost similar to the text of Bāuri Mahārāṇā. It has, however, some passages which are not found in the text of Bāurī Mahārāṇā.

(2) Ms. B.—is called *Bhavanapraveśa.*

It begins thus—

श्री गणेशाए प्रणम्य अविधनभृत्यु इति श्रीन
उमिसारण्ये भुवनप्रवेसे विश्वकर्मामुनिसंवादे।

The Ms. ends abruptly at folio 215 with
वेक पछ हेव 4 चारि अ गु लेखा 8 आठ आगु अला आग हे।

It belongs to a śilpin Śrī Bābāji Mahārāṇā, son of Govinda Mahāṛāṇā of Pathurisāhī, Puri. The original ms. is with him and we are using the copy prepared by my friend Sj. N.K. Bose. Thus ms, among other topics deals with Vāstu and other allied subjects as in A and C.

(3) C—is the printed *Śilpa-śāstra* in Uriyā character published by the Cuttack Printing Company Ltd. 1923. We use this text, as our basis, as it offers the best version available. We have collated A and B with this printed text.

WRITER OF THE WORK

This Śilpaśāstra is said to be written by Bāurī Mahārāṇā, an inhabitant of Orissa, of whom we know very little. But, is he the real writer of this work? It is very doubtful whether he is the real author of the Sanskrit ślokas of this book. In the Uriyā commentary, which we have omitted from our edition, we have his name mentioned thus :—

द्वितीय अध्या समायत। वाउरी महाराणा कृत।।

This Bāurī Mahārāṇā composed the Śilpalakṣaṇa in verses. He says :

शिल्पलक्षण पदकेते। कहिलि एहा मुँहि गीते।।
सुजने मो दोष न धर। वाउरी महाराणा छार।।

Towards the end of the fourth chapter of the Uriyā commentary, he calls himself Viśvakarman :

कहे वाउरी विश्वकर्मा। सखा मो पुरुष उत्तमा।।
सुजने मो दोष न धर। तुम्भ चरणे सु किंकर।।
जन्मरु भूरुस्य अढइ। केवल आग्रे यदुसांइ।।

Viśvakarman is a general name applied to the artists in Orissa. This Bāurī Mahārāṇā was a Vāiṣṇava, because at the end of the first chapter he says :

कृष्ण चरणे चित्त देइ। वाउरी महाराणा कहि।।

The ms. B mentions विश्वकर्मा मुनिसंवाद in the opening line. Again, in A we have a corrupted śloka which reads thus :

नागस्थान स्थानद्वारे विश्वकर्मा च भाषित।
दोषगुण समासाद्य कथितं वास्तुविस्तरम्।।

According to this śloka, the work is ascribed to Viśvakarman. Are we then to suppose that Viśvakarman is the real author of this work and Bāurī Mahārāṇa only the writer of the Uriyā commentary? It is not possible to establish the authorship of the work to Viśvakarman, but we may take Bāurī

Mahārāṇā as the writer of the Uriyā commentary. He might have collected the Sanskrit ślokas from some older śilpaśāstra and added his own commentary. His titles Mahārāṇā and Viśvakarman imply that he was a śilpin (even the present artists of Puri bear the same titles). As a śilpin he could easily get hold of the Sanskrit texts and make a collection like this. There are many passages in the present work, which are similar to those occuring in other śilpa texts. Thus in the present work we have :

वैशाखे धनरत्नानि ज्येष्ठे मृत्युं विनिर्दिशेत्।
आषाढे धनलाभश्च पशुवृद्धिमवाप्नुयात्।।

In Matsyapurāṇam, we have :

वैशाखे धेनुरत्नानि ज्यैष्ठे मृत्युं तथैव च।
आषाढे भृत्यरत्नानि पशुवर्गमवाप्नुयात्।।

It finds a place also in Viśvakarma prakāśa :

वैशाखे धनरत्नानि ज्येष्ठे मृत्युस्तथैव च।
आषाढे भृत्यरत्नानि पशुवर्जमवाप्नुयात्।।

Again, compare the following of our text :

व्यासेन गुणितं दैर्घ्यमष्टाभि र्भजितं पुनः।

Matsyapurāṇam has :

व्यासेन गुणितं दैर्घ्ये अष्टाभिर्वै हृते तथा।

Again, our text has :

पूर्वप्लवो वृद्धिकरो धनदश्चोत्तरप्लवः।
दक्षिणो मृत्युदश्चैव धनहा पश्चिमप्लवः।।

Yuktikalpataru has :

पूर्वप्लवो वृद्धिकरो धनदश्चोत्तरप्लवः।
दक्षिणे मृत्युदो वास्तु र्धनहा पश्चिमप्लवः।।

Another instance from our text is :

अश्विनी रोहिणी मूला ह्युत्तरात्रयमेव च।
स्वाती हस्तानुराधासु स्थम्भारम्भः प्रशस्यते।।

Matsyapurāṇam has :

अश्विनी रोहिणी मूलोत्तरा त्रयमैन्दवम्।
स्वाती हस्तानुराध च गृहारम्भे प्रशस्यते।।

Our text has :

कृत्तिकाद्यास्तु पूर्वादौ सप्तसप्तोदिताः क्रमात्।
यद्दिशं यस्य नक्षत्रं तत्र तस्य शुभं गृहम्।।

Śrīnivāsadīpikā reads :

कृत्तिकाद्यास्तु पूर्वादौ सप्तसप्तोदिताः क्रमात्।
यद्दिश्यां यस्य नक्षत्रं तत्र तस्य शुभं गृहम्।।

Again, our text gives :

आज्यगन्धा ब्रह्मभूमी रक्तगन्धा च क्षत्रिया।

The Vāstuvidyā reads :

आज्यगन्धा च सा भूमि ब्राह्मणानां प्रशस्यते।
रक्तगन्धा च या भूमिः क्षत्रियाणां प्रशस्यते।।

Lastly, our text has :

आदित्यद्वयरोहिणी मृगशिरा ज्येष्ठा धनिष्ठोत्तरा।
पौष्णी विष्णु मघानुराधगुरुभिः शुद्धैः सुतारान्वितैः।।

सौम्यानां दिवसेऽथ पापरहिते योगेतिरिक्ते तिथौ।
विष्ठित्यक्तदिने वदन्ति मुनयो वेश्मादिकार्यं शुभम्।।

We find its parallel in Yuktikalpataru :

आदित्यद्वयरोहिणी मृगशिरो ज्येष्ठाधनिष्ठोत्तराः।
रेवत्याथ मघानुराधहरिभिः शुद्धैः स्वभावादिभिः।
सौम्यानां दिवसेऽथ पापरहिते योगे विरिक्ते तिथौ।
विष्ठित्यक्तदिने वदन्ति मुनयो वैश्मादिकार्यं शुभम्।।

A comparison of the above passages and others as noted elsewhere, would show that the ideas contained in this book regarding the choice of the vāstū land, enumeration of different kinds of houses and the building of the houses, were not quite novel to the compiler of this Uriyā Śīlpaśāstra. He drew his inspiration from the same source as other compilers of other Śilpaśāstra did, because all of them have declared unhesitatingly that they compiled their books from those of the previous ācāryas. The whole śilpa literature seemed to be floating through ages, which saw the construction of magnificient temples and palaces. That mass of literature at times came to be partially confined into various texts by various writers. This we find not any in the texts of Maya, Viśvakarman and others, but also in other non-technical works as Purāṇas (Matsya, Garuḍa, Agni and Bhaviṣya Purāṇas). Sometimes they found a place also in astronomical works like Bṛhatsaṁhitā and Śrīnivāsadīpikā (in Uriyā characters). It is probable that the compiler of our Śilpaśāstra took his materials from the same source floating mass of Śilpa literature.

We are unable to say anything about the antiquity of the present work. As we donot know who the real writer of the work was, it is useless to speculat about his age. But this much is certain that the tradition, from which he had gathered his materials, is as old as the Matsyapurāṇam, which has approximately been fixed in the Gupta Period. It is interesting to note that that old tradition is still living in the heart of Orissa. When I paid a visit to Mayurbhanja, I came across the living tradition of Śīlpaśāstra there. I happened to meet there a man named Baḍia Pāthar, whose profession was to carry a śilpa book and instruct the interested people in the matter of building their houses. He would go about for months in the neighbouring villages and tell the people of the tradition which had been handed down to him by his fathers. I found with him a printed *Śilpaśāstra* (in Uriyā character) published from Cuttack. It is the same book that we are editing with the help of two mss. He told me that his *Śilpa pothīs* had been eaten away by the worms, so he had to recourse to the printed text. This is the living tradition, which I happened to come across in Mayurbhanja (Orissa). There are many śilpins still in Puri, Yajpura, and Bhuvaneśvara, who are even now handing down that old tradition.

SUMMARY OF THE WORK :

Our book begins with an invocation to the god Gaṇeśa. The writer professes to compile this work for the benefit of the whole world. In the first chapter, the theory of Vāstu, which is divided into four kinds, namely, the Brāhmin, Kṣatriya, Vaiśya and Śūdra lands.

The compiler then says how to examine the Vāstu land, whether the land is auspicious or not by making a hole and placing a light in it. There are 16 kind of Vāstu land, namely :

(1) आयतं (2) चतुरस्त्रं
(3) छत्रं (4) भद्रासनं
(5) चक्रं (6) विषमवाहु:
(7) त्रिकोणं (8) शकटाकृति:
(9) दण्डं (10) प्रणवं
(11) मूर्त्ति (12) गृहदं
(13) व्यजनं (14) कूर्मकं
(15) धनुराकारं (16) सूर्यकं।

Then the effect of these lands on the householder are enumerated. He then goes on to specify the time for the beginning of a house and effect each month will produce. The result of building a house on a particular tithi, day or nakṣatra is also mentioned. In the second chapter, eight kinds of Gṛha-bandha as well as their respective effects are enumerated :

(1) ध्वज (2) धूम्र
(3) सिंह (4) श्वा
(5) वृष (6) खर
(7) गज (8) ध्वांक्ष।

The Vāstu-nāga with its eight parts is then described. Then follows an enumeration as to which part of the Nāga is auspicious or not. The third chapter deals with the laying of *sutra* for the construction of the house. The fourth chapter deals with the foundation of the auspicious column and the trees to be planted in the compound of the house. The last chapter is about the ceremony of entering the house when it is completed. Here the printed text does not give the Sanskrit ślokas, but only the Uriyā commentary. The Sanskrit ślokas are found in ms. A only in a corrupted form. So, we have only given the Uriyā verses with their English translation.

Our thanks are due to Mr. N.K. Bose, M.A. for his valuable help, to Pandit Kapileswar Misra for his kind suggestion.

Adikutir Phanindra Nath Bose
Santiniketan
30th March, 1927

शिल्पशास्त्रम्

प्रथमोऽध्यायः

वास्तुलक्षणम्

हेरम्बमम्बिकापुत्रं[1] विघ्नेशं देवपूजितम्।
नत्वाखिलहितार्थाय शिल्पशास्त्रं करोम्यहम्।। 1।।

Bowing down to Heramba, the son of Ambikā, Vighneśa, respected by gods. I write this Śilpaśāstra for the good of the whole world.

वास्तुलक्षणमाख्यामि यस्य लक्षणमुत्तमम्।
देवासुरमनुष्याणां शुभे कर्माणि कारयेत्।। 2।।

I shall narrate the theory of Vāstu, whose good signs are made in the auspicious works of devas, asuras and men.

सर्वदोषविनिर्मुक्तं सर्वाभिर्वाञ्छितं शुभम्।
प्रणम्य सर्वदेवांश्च वास्तुलक्षणमुच्यते।। 3।।

Saluting all the gods, the theory of Vāstu, which is free from all defects, wished for by all and auspicious, is spoken of.

स्निग्धा[2] स्थिरा सुरभिगुल्मलता सुगन्धा।
शस्ता प्रदक्षिणजला च निवासभूमिः।।

---

(1) A and B omit s. 1, 2, 3, 4 A begins with श्रीगणेशाय नमः। अथ सिल्प लिक्षते। Then follows s. 5. B among other topics deals with the subject matter of this Text. From leaf 34 B begins : वास्तुलक्षण। अथतर प्रवक्षामि। गृहकार्यादि संशयः।

(2) cf : स्निग्धा धीरखा प्रदक्षिणजलोपेताशुबीजोद्रमा।।
(Manuṣyālayacandrikā, ch. 1.17).
स्निग्धा . . . बीजोद्गमा।। (as in the above) Śilparatna, 3.1

नेष्टा विपर्ययगुणा कचकर्करास्थि।
बल्मीक कश्मक विभीतक संकुला च।। 4।।

The Vāstu land should be pleasing, firm, full of sweet smelling bushes and creepers, sweet-scented, broad, have water on all sides. If it has contrary virtues, if it is full of hair, gravel, sand and thorn, it is not auspicious

ब्राह्मणा[1] क्षत्रिया वैश्या शूद्रा भूमिश्चतुर्विधा।
शुक्ला रक्ता तथा पीता कृष्णा वर्णैरिति क्रमात्।। 5।।

Lands are of four kinds, the Brāhmin, Kṣatriya, Vaiśya and Śūdra, which are white, red, yellow and black in colour respectively.

आज्यगन्धा[2] ब्रह्मभूमी[3] रक्तगन्धा[4] च क्षत्रिया[5]।
क्षारगन्धा भवेत[6] वैश्या शूद्रा च पुरीषगन्धजा[7]।। 6।।

The Brāhmin land smells *ghee,* Kṣatriya land blood, Vaiśya land *kṣāra* and the Śūdra land night soil.

---

(1) A reads : ब्रह्म क्षेत्रीं वस शूद्रं शुक्लारक्तापिताय।
कृष्णवर्ण च क्रमेणा अतैव वास्तुलक्षणम्।।

B gives a different corrupt reading :

सितवर्ण ब्राह्मणं चैव रक्तवर्णं च त्रिअंस्तथा।
पितवर्ण भवेस्ये शुद्रादि कृष्णवर्णिका।।

(2) A घृतगन्धो, C अज्ञा० (3 A भवेत् व्रह्म

(4) C रजो (5) A अपि वाहुज

(6) भवे (7) A विष्ठासुगन्धिना

कषाया ब्राह्मणा भूमिरम्ला[1] च क्षत्रिया तथा।
वैश्या[2] ख्याता तथा रिक्ता मधुरा शूद्रजातिजा।। 7।।

The Brahmin land tastes acrid, the Kṣatriya land sour, the Vaiśya land bitter and the Śūdra land sweet respectively.

तिलानां[3] वपने तत्र ज्ञातव्या भूमिजातयः।
त्रिरात्रेणांकुरो[4] यत्र[5] ब्रह्मजातिः[6] प्रकीर्तिता।। 8।।

By sowing tila on the land, one may know the class to which the land belongs. The land, in which the sprout comes out in three nights, is known as the Brāhmin class.

क्षत्रिया[7] पंचमी[8] रात्रैर्वैश्या स्यात्[9] सप्तभिस्तथा।
नवरात्रैश्च[10] शूद्राया अङ्कुरो जायते ध्रुवम्।। 9।।

---

(1) A अम्विला (2) A तिक्त वैस समाक्षाता मधुर शूद्रमेवच।

cf : Viśvakarmaprakāśam : 1, 24-26.

श्वेतरक्ता तथा पीता कृष्णावर्णानुपूर्वतः।। 14।।
सुगन्धा ब्राह्मणी भूमी रक्तगन्धानुक्षत्रिणी।
मधुगन्धा भवेद्वैश्या मद्यगन्धा च शुद्रिणी।। 15।।
मधुरा ब्राह्मणी भूमी कषाय क्षत्रियामना।
अम्ला वैश्या भवेद्भूमिस्तिक्ताशूद्राप्रकीर्त्तिता।। 16।।

(3) A reads : स्वादेन लभते यत्र गन्ध तत्र विनीर्दिशेत।

Its commentary, however, refers to the sowing of tila :
भूमिरे तिल वुणिम सावित्रीमंत्रे। एहा समभूमि करिव।।

(4) A त्रिरात्रं च भवेत् (5) A पत्रं (6) A ब्रोश्वर
(7) A क्षत्रियं (8) A पंचरात्राणि (9) A omits स्यात्।
(10) A reads :नवमो शूद्रविख्यातो एवं भूमि परीक्षिताः।

cf : Viśvakarmaprakāśam : 1, 64-66.

हलाकृष्टे तथोद्देशे सर्ववीजानि वापयेत्।। 64।।
त्रिपंचसप्तरात्रेण न प्ररोहन्ति तान्यपि।
उप्तवीजा त्रिरात्रेण सांकुरा शोभना मही।। 65।।
मध्यमा पंचरात्रेण सप्तरात्रेणानिन्दिता।
तिलान्वा वापयेत्तत्र यवांश्चापि च सर्षपान्।। 66।।

(The sprout comes out) in five nights in the Kṣatriya land, in seven nights in the Vaiśya land and in nine nights in Śūdra land.

स्वजात्या[1] सुखमाप्नोति ब्राह्मणस्य[2] चतुर्भूमि[3]।
क्षत्रियाणां[4] त्रिभुमिः स्याद्वैश्यस्तु द्वयभूमिगः[5]।
शूद्राणामेकभूमिश्च चतुर्जाति[6] र्विधीयते।। 10।।

One would get happiness by living on his own class of land. The Brāhmin may live on all the four classes of lands, the Kṣatriya on three classes of lands, the Vaiśya on two and the Śūdra on one—these are the rules for the four classes.

ब्रह्मजातिं[7] यदा भूमिं लोभादिच्छन्ति[8] क्षत्रियाः।
सर्वे[9] ते निधनं यान्ति शैला[10] वज्राहता इव।। 11।।

When the Kṣatriyas wish for the Brāhmin land through greed, they are killed like hills struck by thunder.

नक्षत्रशुद्ध्या गृहनिर्णयम्

कृत्तिकाद्यास्तु[11] पूर्वादौ सप्तसप्तोदिताः क्रमात्।
यद्दिशं यस्य नक्षत्रं तत्र तस्य शुभं गृहम्।। 12।।

---

(1) B omits this śloka. A स्वजाति (2) A व्रध्मस्य
(3) A चतुरभूमौ (4) A क्षत्रियाय (5) A ० भूमि च
(6) A ० वर्ग।
(7) A reads : जेष्ठश्चैव यदा भूमि वर्णहीन त्रयोनर।
सोऽपि वास्तुविनाशस्तु गृहं जम्बुक रोदिते।।
B. व्राध्मणस।
(8) B क्षत्रिअ प्रिअमीछती (9) B स ततो नीधनो
(10) B यमागती व्रजं सिरि
(11) omitted in A and B. cf : Śrīnivāsadīpikā (p. 164) :
कृत्तिकाद्यस्तु पूर्वादौ सप्तसप्तोदिता क्रमात्।
यद्दिश्यां यस्य नक्षत्रं तत्र तस्य शुभं गृहम्।।

Placing seven (Ṛkṣa) respectively beside Kṛttikā and others from the Eastern side onwards, the direction to which the nakṣatra will be, the house will be auspicious on that direction.

वास्तोर्मध्ये[1] तु विवरं कृत्वा बाहुप्रमाणतः।
दीपं तत्र स्थापयित्वा चिन्तयेत् च फलादिकम्।। 13।।

Making a hole, one cubit in length, in the Vāstu land and placing a lamp there, one should think of the results.

श्रीदा[2] दीपशिखा धूम्रा वृद्धिः प्राचीगता भवेत्।
आग्नेये वेशमदाहः स्याद्याम्ये मृत्युर्न संशयः।। 14।।
नैर्ऋते च भवेद्दुःखं वारुण्ये धननाशनम्।
वायव्ये व्याधिपीड़ा स्यादुत्तरस्यां च सम्पदः।
ऐशान्ये सुखवृद्धिः स्यादित्याशाभागनिर्णयः।। 15।।

If the name is smoke-coloured, it gives fortune, if it goes to the east, it predicts increase, if to the south-east the burning of the house, if to the south certain death, if to the

---

(1) Omitted in A and B.

(2) s. 14-15 omitted in A and B.

cf : Mayamata, 4. 106. 10-11

वास्तुमध्ये ततस्तस्मिन् खानयेद् वसुधातलम्।। 10।।
अरत्निमात्रगम्भीरं चतुरश्रसमन्वितम्।
दिग्भागस्थमसम्भ्रान्तमसंक्षिप्तसमुच्छ्रयम्।। 12।।

cf : Viśvakarmaprakāśa, 1. 63 :

ज्वालयेद्भूपरीक्षार्थसंपूर्णसर्वदिङ्मुखम्।। 63।।
दीप्तापूर्वादि गृह्णीयाद्वर्णानामनुपूर्वशः।

cf : Matsyapurāṇam 253, 14 :

ज्वालयेद्भूपरीक्षार्थं तत् पूर्णे सर्वदिङ्मुखम्।। 24।।
दीप्तौ पूर्वादि गृह्णीयाद्वर्णानामनुपूर्वशः।

south-west sorrow, if to the west disease, if to the north wealth, if to the north-east increase of happiness.

षोडशवास्तुभूमिः

आयतं[1] चतुरस्त्रं[2] च छत्रं[3] भद्रासनं तथा।
चक्रं विषमबाहुः[4] स्यास्त्रिकोणं शकटाकृतिम्।। 16।।
दण्डं च प्रणवं[5] मूर्त्तिं गृहदं व्यजनं तथा।
कूर्मकं धनूराकारं सूर्य्यकं चेति षोडशः।। 17।।

These are the sixteen (kinds of Vāstu land) : Āyata or oblong, caturasra or square, chatra or the shape of an umberlla, bhadrāsana or oblong, cakra or disc-shaped, Viṣamavāhu or long and narrow with two unequal wings, trikoṇa or triangular, Śakaṭākṛti or cart shaped, Daṇḍa or staff like, Praṇava or

(1) A आयतन, B आएतए
(2) A चतुश्रेष्ठ:
(3) A यत्र, B कृत
(4) V विष्णुवाड़
cf : Viśvakarmaprakāśa, 1, 27-30
चतुरस्त्रां द्विपाकारां सिंहोक्षाश्वेभरुपिणीम्।
वृत्तं च भद्रपीठं च त्रिशूलं लिंगसन्निभम्।। 27।।
प्रासादध्वजकुम्भादि देवानामपि दुर्लभाम्।
त्रिकोणां शकटाकारां शूर्पव्यजनसन्निभाम्।। 28।।
मुरजाकारसदृशां सर्पमण्डुकरूपणीम्।
खराजागरसङ्काशाम्वकां चिपिढरूपिणीम्।। 29।।
मुद्गराभंतथोलूककाकसर्पनिभां तथा।
शूकरोष्ट्राजसदृशां धनुः परशुरूपिणीम्।। 30।।
cf : Yuktikalpataru, 23, 208-9 :
त्रिकोणो वर्त्तुलो दीर्घो यवमध्यो वृहन्मुखः।।
तथा डमरुरूपश्च सर्पाकारस्तथैवच।
छिन्नो भिन्नो मध्यनिम्नो व्यजनाभश्चतुष्पथः।।
(5) A प्रणवस्थान, B प्रलम्व
After this A has
सुरिक्त वृहामुख व्यजन कूर्मपृष्टः धनु सूर्यचक्र।
B reads प्रलम्व मृछन्द हर्म्यपिढ कृमपृष्ट धनर्यय।

quadrangular, mūrti, gṛhada, vayjana or like a palmleaf fan, kūrmaka or circular, bow-shaped and Sūryaka.

भूमिशुभाशुभफलम्

आयते[1] सिध्यते[2] सर्वं चतुरस्त्रे धनागमः।
छत्रे[3] प्रीतिविवृद्धिश्च भद्रासने कृतार्थिनः[4]।। 18।।
चक्रे दारिद्र्यरोगो[5] च शोको[6] विषमवाहुके।
राजभीति[7]स्त्रिकोणे स्यात् शकटे[8] च धनक्षयम्।। 19।।
चौरा[9] नश्यन्ति दण्डेन प्रणवे नेत्रनाशनम्[10]।
सुमूर्त्तौ[11] म्रियते भार्या गृहदे सुखनाशनम्।। 20।।
व्यजने[12] वित्तनाशश्च[13] धनलाभ[14]श्चकच्छपे।
चापे चौरभयं विद्याद् भास्करे च दरिद्रता।। 21।।

The *Āyata* ensures success, the square brings money, the *chatra* increases love, the *bhadrāsana* fulfills all desires, the *cakra* causes poverty and disease, the Viṣamabāhuka bereavement, the triangular brings fear from the king, the *Śakaṭ a* loss of wealth. The daṇḍa causes the destruction of thieves, the *Praṇava* of eyes, the *Sumūrti* of the wife, the *gṛhada* of happiness, the fan of wealth, the tortoise-shaped brings money. The arrow brings fear of thief and Sūrya brings poverty.

---

(1) A आयतने (2) B सर्वसिद्धि च (3) A क्षत्रपुष्टिविवर्धनं, B कृतिपुष्टविवर्धनं (4) A कृतार्थश्च।
(5) ० मेवोक्तम्, B omits रोगो। (6) ठ वसवाड़ तपाइनं
(7) A नृप० B ० भय। (8) B शकटाधि
(9) A नश्यति चिखो दण्ड, B पशुहोत्रि तयादण्डं।
(10) A क्षयलोचनं, B प्रलम्बे चेष्ठनाशनं (11) A सुरिक्ते प्रियते
(12) B व्यज्ञाने (13) A विनाशं च, B विद्यानाशं च।
(14) A कूर्मे च धनपिड़ते, B कृमेन धनपिडनं।
(15) A चापे धनभयं जातं सूर्ये अन्नक्षयं भवेत्।
B शुर्ये धनक्षयादित धनु चौर भवे मृत्युं।

वैशाखे[1] धनरत्नानि ज्येष्ठे[2] मृत्युं विनिर्दिशेत्।
आषाढे धनलाभश्च[3] पशुवृद्धिमवाप्नुयात्।। 22।।
श्रावणे भूमिलाभः[4] स्याद्धानिर्भाद्रपदे[5] तथा।
पत्नी[6]नाशश्चाश्विने च बहुभार्याश्च[7] कार्त्तिके।। 23।।
मार्गशीर्षे धनप्राप्तिः[8] पौषे चौरभयं[9] तथा।
अशुभं[10] च भयं विद्यादग्निं माघे विनिर्दिशेत्।
फाल्गुने कांचनं पुत्रं[11] चैत्रे च शोकवान्[12] भवेत्।। 24।।

(If a house is begun) in the month of Vaiśākha, wealth and jewels are to be gained, in Jeṣṭha death, in Āṣāḍha gain

---

(1) B has this śloka in leaf 48. Both A and B begin with the month of Caitra and not Vaiśākha.

(2) A येष्टेन पशुचौर्या च।

(3) A धनपशुवृद्धि० B पशुनाशन०

cf : Matsyapurāṇam, 253, 2-5 :

चैत्रे व्याधिमवाप्नोति यो गृहं कारयेन्नरः।
वैशाखे धेनुरत्नानि ज्यैष्ठे मृत्युं तथैव च।। 2।।
आषाढे भृत्यरत्नानि पशुवर्गमवाप्नुयात्।
श्रावणे भृत्यलाभंतु हानिं भाद्रपदे तथा।। 3।।
पत्नीनाशोऽश्विने विन्द्यात् कार्त्तिके धनधान्यकम्।
मार्गशीर्षे तथा भक्तं पौषे तस्करतो भयम्।। 4।।
लाभं च बहुशो विन्द्यादग्निं माघे विनिर्दिशेत्।
फाल्गुने कांचनं पुत्रानिति कालवलं स्मृतम्।। 5।।

cf : Yuktikalpatru, p. 32 :

वैशाख-श्रावणाषाढ मार्गफाल्गुन-कार्त्तिकाः।
सुप्रशस्ता गृहारंभे पत्नीपुत्र-समृद्धिदाः।। 212।।

(4) A भूमिलाभाय, omits स्यात्, B बहुहानी च

(5) B बहुरोगीनी (6) B जन नस्यन्ति

(7) A धान्यानि, B कार्त्तिके धनलाभक

of wealth and increase of cattle, in Śrāvaṇa gain of land, in Bhādra loss, in Āśvina loss of wife, in Kārtika many wives, in Mārgaśīrṣa getting of wealth, in Pouṣa the fear of thief, in Māgha inauspiciousness, fear and fire, in Phālguna gold and in Caitra sorrow.

---

(8) A धनः, B बहुधन चैव (9) ढस्करं भवेत्

(10) A माघे अग्निभयं कुर्यात्, B माघे बहुसोकं च।

(11) A भवेत्, B बहुपुत्रकं (12) A. शोकमवाप्नोति,
B. व्याधि त्रष्ठन्ति।

cf : Viśvakarmaprakāsa, 2. 17-20 :

अथं समयशुद्धिः।। चैत्रे व्याधिमवाप्नोति यो नवं कारयेद्गृहम्।।
वैशाखे धनरत्नानि ज्येष्ठे मृत्युस्तथैव च।। 17।।

आषाढे भृत्यरत्नानि पशुवर्जमवाप्नुयात्।
श्रावणे मित्रलाभं तु हानिं भाद्रपदे तथा।। 18।।

युद्धं चैवाश्विने मासि कार्त्तिके धनधान्यकम्।
धनवृद्धिर्मार्गशीर्षे पोषै तस्करतो भयम्।। 19।।

माघे त्वग्निभयं विन्द्याल्लक्ष्मीवृद्धिश्च फाल्गुने।
गृहसंस्थापनं सूर्ये मेषस्थे शुभदं भवेत्।। 20।।

cf : Vāstu-Prakaraṇaṁ (Ms. in the Viśvabhāratī Library) 1. 4-6 :

चैत्रमासे गृहारम्भे शोकरोगभयं तथा।
वैशाखे शुभदं विद्याज्ज्येष्ठायां मरणं धनं।। 4।।

आषाढे गोकुलं हंति श्रावणे भृत्यवर्धनम्।
भाद्रपदे प्रजारोग्यायुधं चाश्विने एव च।। 5।।

कार्त्तिके धनलाभं स्याद् मार्गशीर्षे महद्भयम्।
पौषे चाग्निभयविधा माघे च बहुदं सुतः(?)।। 6।।

फाल्गुने रत्नहानिं स्यात् मासानां च शुभाशुभम्।

जन्मराशे:[1] शुभं सूर्यस्त्रिषष्ठदशलाभगः।
द्विपंच नवमोऽपीष्ठ स्त्रयोदशदिनात्[2] परम्।। 25।।

If, the sun is on the *janmarāśī* (birthday star of the householder), it is not auspicious to begin the house. Counting from there, there would be gain on the third, sixth and tenth day, as well as on the second, fifth, ninth and thirteenth day.

तिथिशुद्धिः

गृहं[3] कृत्वा प्रतिपदि दुःखं प्राप्नोति नित्यशः।
अर्थक्षयं तथा षष्ठ्यां[4] पंचम्यां चित्तचांचल्यः।। 26।।

Building a house on *Pratipadā* day one always gets sorrow, on *Śaṣṭhī* day loss of money and on *Pañcamī* day restlessness of mind.

चौरभीति[5] दशम्यां तु चैकादश्यां[6] नृपाद् भयम्।
पत्नीनाशस्तु[7] पौर्णमास्यां स्थाननाशः[8] कुहौ तथा।। 27।।

On *Daśamī,* there would be the fear of thief, on *Ekādaśī* the fear of the king, on *pūrṇimā* the loss of wife, on the new moon day the loss of place.

---

(1) A यत्रराशिस्थितं सूर्यः त्रिषष्ठदशलाभकं एकादश।
B omits the śloka.

(2) A विनात्। A has some ślokas on रविशुद्धिः, वारशुद्धिः and वारफलम्।

(3) B omits śloka 26. A. प्रतिपद गृहकार्यं च

(4) A षष्टि पंचमोकाठनं तथा।

(5) B omits this śloka. A ०भय (6) A एकादशीद्वादशीनृपाभयात्।

(7) A नाशं च

(8) A पतिनाशो कुहुस्तथा।

रिक्तायां[1] सर्वकार्यानि नाशमायान्ति सर्वदा।
द्वितीया सप्तमी चैव तृतीयाष्ट त्रयोदशी।।
पंचसु[2] स्तम्भकर्माणि स्थिरलग्ने शुभे क्षणे।। 28 ।।

On the *riktā tithis* (i.e., चतुर्थी, नवमी and चतुर्दशी) all work always tend to destruction. On these five—*dvitīyā, saptamī, tṛtīyā, aṣṭamī* and *trayodaśī* at auspicious moment the column should be placed.

वारफलं

वह्ने[3] र्भयं भवति भानुदिनेऽर्थनाशः।
सौरेदिने[4] क्षितिसुतस्य च वज्रपातः।। 29 ।।

On Sunday, there is the fear of fire, on monday the loss of money and on Tuesday the falling of thunder.

प्रासादसद्मपुर–पुष्करिणीक्रियासु।
धर्मार्थवांछितफलानि शुभग्रहाणाम्[6] ।। 30 ।।

In the work of palace, house, city and tanks, the auspicious planets (produce) results desired by dharma and artha.

नक्षत्रफलं

आदित्यद्वयरोहिणीमृगशिराज्येष्ठा[7] धनिष्टोत्तरा।
पौष्णी[8] विष्णु मघानुराधगुरुभिः[9] शुद्धैः[10] सुतारान्वितैः[11] ।। 31 ।।

These are the pure and auspicious stars—āditya, dvaya, Rohiṇi, Mṛgaśirā, Jyeṣṭhā, Dhaniṣṭottarā, Pauṣṇī, Viṣṇu and Maghā.

(1) A omits this line, B omits ślokas 27-35.
(2) A पंचेते धनरत्नानि स्थम्भ शुभे क्षणे।
(3) A वदेयं (4) A ० रपि (5) A ० घातः।
(6) A ० ग्रहानि (7) A ० शिरो (8) A पौष्य
(9) A मृगा ० (10) A शुद्धे (11) A सुपुत्रान्विजयते।

सौम्यानां दिवसेऽथ[1] पापरहिते योगोऽतिरिक्ते तिथौ।
विष्टित्यक्तदिने वदन्ति मुनयो वेश्मादिकार्यं[2] शुभम्[3] ।। 32 ।।

Sages say that the building of houses is auspicious on the days of moon, on sinless yoga, an extra tithi and on days which are not connected with Visti.

(अन्यच्च) अश्विनी रोहिणी मूला ह्युत्तरात्रयमेवच।
स्वाती हस्तानुराधासु स्तम्भारम्भः प्रशस्यते।। 33 ।।

(Otherwise) it is advisible to begin the column with the following stars : Aśvinī, Rohiṇī, Mūla, Uttarā, Svātī, Hastā and Anurādhā.

धनुर्मीनद्वयोर्मध्ये[4] यावत्तिष्ठति चन्द्रमाः।
न छिन्द्यात्तृणकाष्ठादीन्न गच्छेद्दक्षिणां दिशम्।। 34 ।।

When the moon rests between Dhanuḥ and Mīna, no one should cut grass, wood and other things and no one should go to the south.

विश्वेदेवे चाग्निभयं श्रावणायां भयं भवेत्।
धनिष्ठायां भवेद्रोगो वरुणे मरणं ध्रुवम्।
अजपादे नृपभयं जातं शरणपंचके।। 35 ।।

---

(1) A अपाप० (2) A कार्य (3) A शुभा।

cf : Yuktikalpatarum p. 32, s. 217.

आदित्यद्वयरोहिणी मृगशिरो ज्येष्ठाधनिष्ठोत्तराः।
रेवत्याथ मधानुराधहरिभिः शुद्धैः स्वभावादिभिः।
सौम्यानां दिवसेऽथ पापरहिते योगेविरिक्ते तिथौ।
विष्टित्यक्तदिने वदन्ति मुनयो वेश्मादिकार्यं शुभम्।। 217 ।।

cf : Matsyapurāṇam : 253, 6 :

अश्विनी रोहिणी मूलोत्तरा त्रयमैन्दवम्।
स्वाती हस्तोऽनुराधा च गृहारम्भे प्रशस्यते।। 6 ।।

(4) A omits ślokas 33-36.

In the month of Āṣaḍa, there is the fear of fire, in Śrāvaṇa fear, in Dhaniṣṭhā disease, in Varuṇa certain death, in Ajapāda fear of king,—these are the Śaraṇapañcaka.

जन्मचन्द्रः श्रियं कुर्याद्वर्जयेत् पंचकर्मसु।
यात्रा युद्धे गृहारम्भे भैषज्ये पशुसंग्रहे।। 36।।

The birthday moon (ordinarily) does good, but it should be avoided in the following five cases—in going elsewhere, in war, in beginning a house, in medicine and in collection of animals.

जन्मतारे भवेत् क्लेशः सम्पदि सुखसम्पदः।
विपदि कार्यनाशः स्यात् क्षेमेण क्षेमलाभकः।। 37।।
प्रत्यरौ परमं रोगं साधके सर्वसाधकः।
निधने धनहानिश्च मैत्रे परममंगलम्।। 38।।

The birthday star brings suffering, with sampada there would be happiness and wealth, with vipada loss of work, with kṣema attainment of good, with pratyari fatal disease, with sādhaka fulfillment of all, with nidhana loss of wealth, with maitra great good.

सप्ताद्यचन्द्रे ध्रुवमर्थलाभः।
षष्ठे तृतीये धनभोगमायुः।
सर्वार्थसिद्धिं दशमे वदन्ति।
एकादशे सर्वसुखानि चैव।। 39।।

With the seventh birthday moon, there would be certain gain of money, with the sixth and third wealth, enjoyment and long life, with the tenth attainment of all ends, with the eleventh attainment of all kinds of happiness.

द्वितीयोऽध्यायः

गृहबन्धः

व्यासेन[1] गुणितं दैर्घ्यमष्टाभि र्भाजितं पुनः।
शेषं ध्वजादिकं ज्ञेयं पूर्वादिभवनाष्टके।। 1।।

If the length is multiplied by breadth and again divided by eight, the remainder is known respectively as Dhvaja and others in eight kinds of houses.

ध्वजो[2] धूम्रश्च[3] सिंहश्च[4] श्वा[5] वृष खर एव[6] च।
गजो[7] ध्वांक्षतथैतानि गृहबन्ध स उच्यते।। 2।।

---

(1) A reads :
विस्ताराणि हस्तं च प्रतिराशि दूसं च कारयेत्।
अष्टाभि हरते भागे शेषबन्ध स उच्यते।।
B has a corrupt reading.
cf : Matsyapurāṇam, 257, 15-16.
व्यासेन गुणिते दैर्घ्ये अष्टाभि र्वै हृते तथा।। 15।।
यच्छेषमायतं विन्द्यादष्टभेदं वदामि वः।
ध्वजो धूमश्च सिंहश्च वृषभः खर एव च।। 16।।
हस्ती ध्वांक्षश्च पूर्वाद्याः कशेषाभवन्त्यमी।

(2) A ध्वजे (3) A धूम च
(4) A सिंहायु
(5) A श्यान (6) A स्तथा
(7) A ध्वासायते चैव
B reads : श्री ध्वज धूम्र। सिंह। श्वन्। वृष।
खर। गज। ध्वज। 8। ए अष्टबन्ध।।
cf : Yuktikalpataru, p. 45 :
ध्वजो धूमस्तथा सिंहः श्वावृषो गर्दभो गजः।
काक इत्येष गदितो वास्तुस्थानस्य निर्णयः।
cf : Vāstuvidyā, p. 21-22 :
ध्वजः सिंहो वृषो हस्ती महादिग्देवताः ह्यमूः।। 21।।
विदिङ्नाथास्तु धूमः श्वा खरो ध्वाङ्क्ष इति स्मृताः।
cf : मनुष्यालयचन्द्रिका, p. 16, s. 16 :
ध्वजधूमसिंहकुक्कुरवृषखरगजवायसाः क्रमेण स्युः।

These are called Gṛhabandhas : Flag, dhūmra, lion, dog, buffalo, ass, elephant and crow.

ध्वजे[1] विभूति मरणं च धूम्रे
सिंहे जयः श्वा च करोत्यनर्थम्।
भोगो वृषे हानिकरः खरे च
पुष्टि गर्जे काकपदे च दुःखम्।। 3।।

The dhvaja house brings wealth, the dhūmra house death, the siṁha house victory, the śvā house destruction, the vriṣa house enjoyment, the khara house loss, the gaja house nourishment, the kāka house sorrow.

ध्वजे[2] देवगृहं कुर्याद्[3]धूम्रे[4] च होमशाल[5]कम्।
सिंहे[6] च श्रीगृहं[7] कुर्यात्[8] शुनि कुट्टणिशालकम्।। 4।।

---

cf : Viśvakarmaprakāśa, 2, 49-50 :
विस्तारेण हतं दैर्ध्यं विभजेदष्टभिस्ततः।। 49।।
यच्छेषं संभवेदायो ध्वजाद्यास्ते स्थुरष्टधा।
ध्वजो धूम्रो हरिः श्वागौः खरेभीवायसोष्टमः।। 50।।

(1) Both A and B omit this śloka.
cf : Yuktikalpataru, p. 45, s. 310 :
ध्वजे विभूति र्विपदश्च धूमे
सिंहे विभोगः शुनि सर्वनाशः।
वृषे सुखं गर्दभतो विनाशः
गजे धनं काकपदे मृत्युः।। 310।।

cf : Viśvakarmaprakāśa, 2, 53 :
ध्वजः सिंहे तौ च गजेह्येतेगविशुभप्रदाः।
वृषो नपूजितोह्यत्र ध्वजः सर्वत्रपूजितः।। 53।।

(2) A ध्वजेन (3) A कुर्या (4) A धृमेन, B धूम्रेण
(5) C ० शालकः, B ० शालिका (6) B सिंघेन
(7) A श्रीघरं, B शिरिघरं
(8) B कुर्या, the remaining portion of śloka is omitted in B.

वृषे अन्तःपुरं[1] कुर्यात् खरे पशुन्नि[2]योजयेत्।
गजे भण्डारकं[3] चैव ध्वांक्षे[4] च शस्त्रशालकम्[5] ।। 5।।

With dhvaja a temple should be built, with dhūmra the sacrificial house, with Simha Śrīgṛha (an audience hall), with Śiva the place for crushing rice, with Vṛṣa the inner appartment, with khara a stable, with gaja a store and with dhvāmkṣa an armoury.

अष्टाभि र्गुणितं[7] पिण्डमृक्षभागेन हारयेत्।
शेषमृक्षं[8] विजानीयादश्विन्यादि[9] क्रमेण च।। 6।।

The area (piṇḍa) of the house, multiplied by 8 (the number of Bandha) should be divided by Ṛkṣa (or 27-the number of the stars), the remainder Ṛkṣa star (being the star of the house) should be known respectively as Aśvinī and others.

---

(1) A ० पुर (2) A योजयेत्

(3) A भण्डारकश्चैव (4) A धुम्रेन

(5) C ० शालकः।

(6) B हरते (7) A भोगेन (8) B असं

(9) A ० गुणिते बुधः, B तत्र ऋक्ष वेणी दृस्यते।

cf : Matsyapurāṇam, 257, 20 :
तमेवाष्टगुणं कृत्वा करराशिं विचक्षणः।
सप्तविंशादृते भागे ऋक्षं विद्याद्विचक्षणः।। 20।।

cf : Garuḍapurāṇam, 46, 27 :
अष्टाभि र्गुणितं पिण्डं षष्टिभिः र्भागहारितम्।
यच्छेषन्तद् भवेज्जीवं मरणं भूतहारितम्।। 27।।

cf : Śrīnivāsadīpikā, 7, p. 166 :
व्यासेन गुणिते दैर्घ्ये वसुभि र्विहृते ततः।।
तच्छेषमायतं विद्यात् पूर्वादिभवनाष्टके।।

वसुभि[1] र्गुणितं पिण्डं[2] षष्टिभागेन हारयेत्।
शेषमंशं[3] विजानीयादायुर्गेहस्य[4] कोविदः।। 7।।

If the area is multiplied by 8 and divided by 60, the learned should know that the remainder is the *Āyuṣ* (duration) of the house.

पृथिवीजलतेजांसि वायुराकाश एव च।
पंचभूतायते[5] तत्र भग्नं[6] दाहादि जायते।। 8।।

If the remainders are the five elements—(1) earth, (2) water, (3) heat, (4) air and (5) sky, (the result of the duration of the house) would be destruction, burning etc.

ऋक्षं चतुर्गुणं कुर्यान्न[7]वभागेन हारयेत्।
शेषमंशं[8] विजानीयात्तं लब्धं[9] राशिमादिशेत्।। 9।।

If the Rkṣa (the star of the house) is multiplied by 4 and divided by 9, the remainder should be known as Ṛāśī.

आदौ[10] चौरभयं भोगी द्वितीये वित्तनाशकम्।
वह्नौ वेदे भवेद्दाता नृपतिः पंचमे तथा।। 10।।

---

(1) B omits this śloka A पिण्ड (2) A अष्ठाभिः
(3) A गुणितं बुधः (4) A omits this śloka. B आप
(5) C पंचस्य, B, text is corrupt after this.
(6) A रिख्या (7) A ० नवभि र्भाग B कृत्वा०
(8) A शेषतां (9) A लब्धि
(10) s. 10 is imitted in A, B. has a corrupt Text.

षष्ठे[1] भयमवाप्नोति सप्तमे च नपुंसकः।
वसौ दरिद्रतामेति नवमे विष्णुमन्दिरम्।। 11।।

If the remainder is one, there would be fear of thief, if two, enjoyment, if three, loss of wealth, if four donor, if five king, if six there would be fear, if seven eunuch, if eight poverty, if nine temple of Viṣṇu.

अष्ठाभि र्भजितादृक्षाद्यच्छेषं स व्ययो भवेत्।
व्ययाधिक्यं न कर्त्तव्यं गृहमायाधिकं शुभम्।। 12।।

That is called *Vyaya* what remains by dividing the Ṛkṣa (star of the house) by eight. A house should not be made such as having excess of vyaya, if it has excess of āya, it is auspicious.

नागप्रमाणम्

ऋक्षेण[2] गुणितं पिण्डं अष्टभागेन हारयेत्।
अष्टौ नागाननन्तादीन् भागशेषं प्रकल्पयेत्।। 13।।

Piṇḍa multiplied by Ṛkṣa (star of the house) should divided by eight. The remainder indicates the eight (vāstu)

---

(11) s. 11-12 omitted in A and B.

cf : Matsyapurāṇam, 257, 21 :

अष्ठभि र्भाजिते ऋक्षे यः शेषः स व्ययो मतः।
व्ययाधिक्यं न कुर्बीत यतो दोषकरं भवेत्।।

cf : Garuḍapurāṇam, 46, 25-26 :

पुनर्गुणितमष्टाभि र्ऋक्षभागंतु भाजयेत्।
यच्छेषं तद्भवेदृक्षं भागै र्हत्वा व्ययं भवेत्।। 25।।
ऋक्षं चतुर्गुणं कृत्वा नवभिर्भागहारितम्।
शेषमंशं विजानीयाद्देवलस्य मतं यथा।। 26।।

cf : Śrīnivāsadīpikā, p. 167 :

वसुशिष्टं तथायातं नक्षत्रं भवति व्ययः।।
व्ययाधिकं न कर्त्तव्यं गृहमायाधिकं शुभम्।।

(2) cf : A and B omits s. 13.

nāgas, Ananta (Vāsuki, Takṣaka) and others.

बालाग्र[1]कलिकादर्भयूकसूत्र[2]पदाः क्रमात्।
चतुर्गुणानि कृत्यैता[3]न्यंगूलीः कथयन्ति[4] हि।। 14।।

Angulis are said to be four times respectively of the point of hair, kalikā, darbha, yuka and sūtrapada.

यथा पृथ्वी तथा वास्तु यथा वास्तु तथा मही।
स्थाने स्थाने प्रकल्पन्तें[5] विपाके[6] नाग[7] अन्तकः।। 15।।

What is earth is Vāstu, what is Vāstu is earth. The Nāga Antaka should be imagined as places.

वास्तुनागविचारः

भद्रादौ[8] तु शिरः पूर्वे मार्गादौ[9] दक्षिणे शिरः।
फाल्गुनादौ[10] शिरः प्रत्यक् ज्येष्ठादावुत्तरे शिरः।। 16।।

In the Bhādra and following months, the head of the (Vāstu) nāga rests on the East, in the Mārgaśīrṣa and following months on the South, in the Phālguna and following months on the West and on Jyeṣṭha and following on the North.

---

(1) B omits s. 14-15. A वसीकाद्याभे, s. 14 has no connection with the previous or following ślokas.

(2) A ०पादानि च (3) A ०स्मिन्यंगुल

(4) A जनयति (5) A परिकूपे

(6) A विपाक (7) A नागनन्तक

(8) B omits s. 16-18. A पूर्वे शिर भाद्रवार्द्धे

(9) A मार्गे दक्षिणमस्तके (10) फाल्गुणे वारुणेन्धेसे

(11) A जेष्ठे उत्तरमूर्द्धणि

cf : Śrīnivāsadīpikā, p. 165 :

पूर्वादिक्षु शिरः कृत्वा नागः शेते त्रिभिस्त्रिभिः।
भाद्राद्यौ वामपार्श्वेन तस्य क्रोड़े शुभं गृहम्।।

शिरसा पृष्टपुच्छाभ्यामशुभं[1] च भवेद् गृहम्।
शयन[2] वामपार्श्वेन तस्य क्रोड़े शुभं भवेत्[3]।। 17।।

A house on its head, back and tail is inauspicious, but it is auspicious on its left side and on its lap.

शिरः[4] प्रदेशापुच्छान्तं नागदीर्घं च स्थापयेत्।
अष्टभागै र्हतं तस्य लब्धं तालं विदुर्बुधाः।। 18।।

The length of the house should be the length of the (Vāstu) nāga from its head to tail. The length divided by eight is known to the learned as tāla.

अष्टभागकृता[5] भूमिः प्रथमं शिरः उच्यते।
द्वितीये हृदयं चैव तृतीये जठरं तथा।। 19।।

चतुर्थं नाभिकं विन्द्याद्पंचमं गुह्यमेव च।
षष्ठं स्याज्जानुदेशं च सप्तमं जघनं तथा।। 20।।

The (Vāstu) land being divided into eight parts, the first is called head, the second heart, the third belley, the fourth navel, the fifth scrottum, the sixth thigh and the seventh hip.

---

(1) A ०पुच्छाभ्याः शशुरोतदिगन्तए (2) शयने

(3) A गृहम्।

(4) s. 18 is omitted in A and B.

(5) B omits s. 19-22. A gives a different reading :

तालमेको कण्ठशिरः द्वিताल कण्ठकस्तम्भा।
त्रिभितालहृदयेश्चैव चतुर्तालोदरं भवेत्।।
पंचताल नाभिश्चैव षष्ठताल गुहकस्तथा।
सप्तताल जघनश्चैव अष्टतालश्च पुच्छये।।

दारापत्यप्रणाशो भवति च खनने मस्तके नागराजस्य[1]।
श्रीसम्पत्तिः प्रभुत्वं[2] यदि[3] हृदि जठरे सर्वभागैरुपेतः।। 21।।
नाभिगात्रे[4] रतिशयभयदो गुह्यदेशे च[5] रोगो।
जान्वों[6] दीर्घप्रवासी क्षयमपि[7] जघने पुच्छदेशे च मृत्युः।। 22।।

इति नागपरिमाणसमाप्तिः

If (at the time of building the house) the head (of the Vāstu nāga) is dug, there would be loss of the life of wife and children, but if the heart, attainment of wealth and property and mastery, if the belley, all kinds of enjoyment, if the navel, great fear, if scrottum disease, if thigh long absence from house, if hip decay, if tail death.

(1) नागराज्जिज्ञा, C नागरांकः।
(2) A प्रभुका (3) C हृदय
(4) A त्वरातेरतिशशुभदोनाभौक्षीणं (5) A भोगं
(6) A जानु (7) A खलु

तृतीयोऽध्यायः

सूत्रलक्षणम्

ध्वजवस्त्रपताकादि[1] दर्शने धनसंभवः।
पूर्णकुम्भे भवेत् वित्तं प्राप्नोति कनकादिकम्।। 1।।

In laying the thread for the foundation of the house, at the sight of flag, cloth and other things, there is possibility of gaining wealth and at the sight of a full pitcher of wealth, gold and other things.

शत्रुंक्षयं वाद्यघोषे वेदघोषे भवेच्छुभम्।
ज्योतिः शास्त्रकथायां तु वर्द्धते गृहिणो धनम्।। 2।।

At the sound of drum, there would be destruction of enemy, at the chanting of the Vedas, there would be good and at the reading of the *jyotis-śāstra*, the wealth of the householder increases.

हीनांगो भिक्षुकश्चैव बन्ध्या रोगार्त्तिखंजकौ।
दृश्यते चेद्गृहारम्भे कर्त्तुश्च मरणं ध्रुवम्।। 3।।

If at the time of beginning the house, a crippled, a beggar, a barren woman, a diseased person and a lame man are seen, the owner's death is certain.

---

(1) s. 1-4 omitted in A and B.

सूत्रस्य[1] छेदनात् क्षिप्रं दुःखं स्यान्मरणान्तकम्।
अतो विधिविधानेन शान्तिहोमं तु कारयेत्।। 4।।

If the thread tears, there would be sorrow amounting to death, therefore, *śānti-homa* should be performed according to the proper rules.

सूत्रे[2] विस्तीर्यमाने[3] तु रोदनं[4] श्रूयते[5] यदि[6]।
नाभिमाने[7] स्थितं[8] शल्यं मुण्डमालां विनिर्दिशेत्।। 5।।

सूत्रे[9] विस्तीर्यमाने[10] तु गजशब्दो[11] यदा भवेत्।
गजस्यास्थि[12] विजानीयाद्वास्तुभूमौ न संशयः।। 6।।

सूत्रे विस्तीर्यमाने तु ध्यशब्दो[13] यदा भवेत्।
तत्राश्वास्थि विजानीयाद्धनहानि भवेदध्रुवम्।। 7।।

---

(1) cf : Matsyapurāṇam, 256, 21 :
सूत्रछेदे भवेन्मृत्युर्व्याधिः कीले त्वधोमुखे।
अङ्गारेषु तथोन्मादं कपालेषु च सम्भ्रमम्।। 21।।
cf : Śrīnivāsadīpikā, p. 169 :
सूत्रच्छेदे भवेन्मृत्युः कीले च वाङ्मुखे महान् रोगः।
गृहनाथस्थपतिनां स्मृतिलोपे मृत्युरावेशः।
cf : Bṛhat Saṁhitā, 53, 110 :
सूत्रच्छेदे मृत्युः कीले चात्राङ्मुखे महान् रोगः।
गृहनाथस्थपतीनां स्मृतिलोपे मृत्युरादेश्यः।। 220।।

(2) B शुत्र, A सुत्र (3) A विस्तार्यमानस्तु, B विस्तारमानेन

(4) A रोदिते, B मानवशब्द (5) A श्वासते, B शुभे (6) A अथवा

(7) ०मात्र, B वर्यएतए भूमि सा। मरण तत्र निसंसयः।

(8) A स्थिते (9) A सुत (10) A विस्तार्यमानस्तु

(11) A ध्वनिमुदामृत (12) A गज अस्थि

(13) B omits s. 7 A. ध्वानिमुदाहृतं

(14) A ध्यय अस्थि, विजानिया सन्त तिष्ठति नान्यथा।

If at the time of laying the thread, the cry is heard, the śalya-a garland of heads is pointed out at the navel, or if the elephant's sound is heard, elephant's bone should be known to exist in Vāstu land without doubt, or if the horse's neigh is heard, horse's bone should be known to exist and there would certainly the loss of wealth.

सूत्रे विस्तीर्यमाने तु धेनुः[1] शब्दायते[2] यदि।
गवास्थीन्यत्र जानीया[3]न्मृत्यु[4] र्वास्तुपते भवेत्।। 8।।
सूत्रे[5] विस्तीर्यमाने तु कुक्कुरो यदि रुद्येत्।
अचिरेणैव कालेन शूना निहत एव सः।। 9।।

If at the time of laying the sūtra, cow's lowing is heard, cow's bone should be known to exist there and the death of the lord of Vāstu would follow, or if the dog barks, he would soon be killed by the dog.

गर्दभो[6] शब्द्यते यत्र तद्गेहं परिवर्जयेत्।
काको दृष्ट्वा मुखं रौति ध्रुवं मृत्यु र्विनिर्दिशेत्।। 10।।

---

(1) A गवाय (2) A रोदन्ते

(3) A गोऽअस्थि (4) A विजानीय०।

(5) A मृत्ये वास्तु यथार्थजा।

(6) A and B omits this śloka.

cf : Matsyapurāṇam, 256, 19-20.
प्रसार्यमाणे सूत्रे तु श्वा गोमायु र्विलंघते।
तत् तु शल्यं विजानीयात् खरशब्देऽतिभैरवे।। 19।।
यदीशाने तु दिगभागे मधुरं रौति वायसः।
धनं तत्र विजानीयाद्भागे वा स्वाम्यधिष्ठिते।। 20।।

(7) B omits s. 9-10. A reads :
गर्धवो यस्य स्यात् परिवर्जयेते रोदन्ते।
पुत्रकालस्तु ध्रुव मृत्यु विनिर्दिशेत्।।

Where an ass brays, that hould should be vacated. If a crow caws seeing the face, it signifies certain death.

सूत्रे विस्तीर्यमाने तु पन्नगो[1] यदि दृश्यते।
अचिरेणैव कालेन सर्पेण[2] निहतो ध्रुवम्।। 11।।

If at the time of laying the sūtra a serpent is seen, he would certainly be soon killed by a serpent.

---

(1) A पनंगो

(2) स्वामी न हत पनग।

cf : Bṛhat Saṁhitā : 53, 108 :
सूत्रे प्रसार्यमाणे गर्दभरावोऽस्थिशल्यमाचष्टे।
श्वशृङ्गांललंघिते वा सूत्रे शल्यं विनिर्देश्यम्।। 208।।

B adds : सूत्रे प्रसार्यमाने शङ्खशब्दं श्रूयते यदि।
देवभूमि र्भवेत् सा ताम्मानवो वर्जयेत् सदा।।
सूत्रे विस्तीर्यमाने तु शिलाघातो भवेत् यदि।
वर्जयेत् तादृशीं भूमिं जननाशः भवेत् सदा।

चतुर्थोऽध्याय:

मंगलारोचनविधि:

भस्मास्थि काष्ठ[1]मंगारं तुषं वालं कपालकम्।
रक्त[2]पुत्तिकदन्तं च मृद्भाण्डास्थीनि यत्र वै।
तत्रावासो न कर्त्तव्य: कृते कीर्त्तिधनक्षयम्।। 1।।

इष्टकायामर्थलाभ:[3] पाषाणे सर्वसम्पद:।
सर्पादौ निधनं कर्त्तुरंगारे च कुलक्षयम्।। 2।।

If (from the hole of the auspicious column) ash, bone, wood, burnt wood, husk, blood, tooth, earthenpot, come out, one should not live in such a place. If one lives there, he would lose his dharma and glory. If brik comes out there would be gain of wealth, if stone, all kinds of property, if serpent and others, the death of the householder, if burnt wood, loss of family.

---

(1) B omits s. 1-3. A ०दुस्थतु केशकपोलदण्डरक्त।

(2) A. gives a corrupt reading :
सर्व यदि वाथ शिला च लोष्ठे धर्मकुल।
मलिनीकलाज नाना तस्मिन् वदन्ति मुनयो धर्मकीर्त्तिनाशम्।।

(3) s. 2. does not occur in A. s. 3. comes after many, ślokas.

(4) A करोवृद्धि (5) A उत्तरे धनहा

(6) A पश्चिमे धनसाशाय दक्षिणे मृत्युरेवच।।
cf : Yuktikalpatru, s. 304 b, 305 a.
पूर्वप्लवो वृद्धिकरो धनश्चोत्तरप्लव:।। 304।।
दक्षिणे मृत्युदो वास्तु धनहा पश्चिमप्लव:।।

गृहवृद्धिः

पूर्वप्लवो वृद्धिकरो[4] धनद[5]श्चोत्तरप्लवः।
दक्षिणो[6] मृत्युदश्चैव धनहा पश्चिमप्लवः।। 3।।

Extension of the house on the East signifies increase, on the north giving of money, on the South death and on the West losing of wealth.

पूर्वेऽश्वत्थं[1] वर्जयित्वा तिंतडीं दक्षिणे तथा।
पश्चिमांशे वटं तद्वदुत्तरे न ह्युदुम्वरम्।। 4।।

The Aśvattha tree should be avoided on the East, the tamarind on the South, the banyan on the West and fig tree on the north.

---

(1) In A these ślokas occur towards the end.
A's version is a little different :
वर्जयेत् वा पूर्वे अश्वत्थं दक्षिणे पलाशस्तथा।
न्यग्रोध पश्चिमे भागे उत्तरस्तु भद्रम्वर।।

(2) A इशाने B इशान्ये (3) A अग्निया, B अग्निए

(4) A कण्टकी, B कण्टिको (5) A शिमुली।
cf : मनुष्यालयचन्द्रिका, 1, 22.
पूर्वस्यां वकुलो वटश्च शुभदोऽवाच्यां तथोदुम्बर-
श्चिञ्चा चाम्बुपतौ तु पिप्पलतरुः सप्तच्छदोऽपि स्मृतः।
कौवेर्यां दिशि नागसंज्ञिततरुः प्लक्षश्च संशोभनाः
प्राच्यादौ तु विशेषतः पनसपूगौ केरचूतौ क्रमात्।।
cf : शिल्परन्तम्, 3. 21-22 :
अश्वत्थः पूर्वतो धन्यो दक्षिणे चाप्युदुम्बरः।
न्यग्रोधः पश्चिमे प्लक्षोऽपयुत्तरेति परे जगुः।। 21।।
पूर्वाद्युदुम्बराश्वत्थाप्लक्षन्यग्रोधकास्तु वा।
सर्वत्र केसराश्चूताः पुन्नागा नागडाडिमाः।। 22।।

ऐशान्ये रक्तपुष्पं च आग्नेये क्षीरपादपम्।
नैऋते कण्टकं चैव वायव्ये शाल्मलीं तथा।। 5।।

The red flower trees should be avoided on the north-east, the Kṣīra trees (fig trees) on the south-east and the thorny trees on the south-west and the silk cotton tree on the west.

शुभवृक्षाः

यत्रतत्र स्थिता वृक्षा विल्वदाडिम्बूकेशराः।
पनसो नारिकेलं च शुभं कुर्वन्ति नित्यशः।। 6।।

Where there are Bilva, pomegranete, keśara, jack-fruit, coconut trees, they always do good.

---

cf : Vāstuvidyā, 2, 33-6 :
वर्णक्रमेणाथ विद्याद् वृक्षान् शास्त्रविशारदः
अश्वत्थ पूर्वतो धन्यो दक्षिणे च उदुम्बरः।। 33।।
न्यग्रोधः पश्चिमे श्रेष्ठः प्लक्षोऽत्त्युत्तरतः शुभः।
न्यग्रोधः पूर्वतो वर्ज्यो दक्षिणे प्लक्ष एव च।। 34।।
अश्वत्थः पश्चिमे भागे उत्तरे चाप्युदुम्बरः।
अश्वत्थोऽग्निभयं कुर्यात् प्लक्षः कुर्यात् प्रमादकम्।। 35।।
न्यग्रोधः शस्त्रसम्पातं कुक्षिरोमुदुम्बरः।
काष्टेष्टकातुषांगारपाषाणास्थः सरीसृपान्।। 36।।
cf : Garuḍapurāṇam, 46, 36 :
अश्वत्थप्लक्षन्यग्रोधः पूर्वादौ स्यादुडुम्बरः।
गृहस्य शोभनः प्रोक्त ईशाने चैव शाल्मलिः।।

(1) A and B omit s. 6-7.
cf : Matsyapurāṇam, 225, 20-24 :
भवनस्य वटः पूर्वे दिग्भागे सर्वकामिकः।
उदुम्बरस्तथा याभ्ये वारुण्यां पिप्पलः शुभः।। 20।।
प्लक्षश्चोत्तरतो धन्यो विपरीतास्त्वसिद्धये।
कण्टकी क्षीरवृक्षश्च असनः सफलो द्रुमः।। 21।।

प्रागादिस्ये[1] सलिले सुतहानिः शिखिभयं रिपुभयं च।
स्त्रीकलहः स्त्रीदौष्ट्यं नैःष्टं वित्तमृज वृद्धिः।। 7।।

If there is water on the East, there would be the loss of son, fear of fire (on the South-east) fear of enemy (on the South), quarrel with wife (on the West), naughty wife (on the South-west) and no increase of wealth (on the West).

भार्याहानौ प्रजाहानौ भवेतां क्रमशस्तदा।
न छिन्द्याद् यदि तानन्यनन्तरे स्थापयेच्छुभान्।। 22।।
पुन्नागाशोकवकुलशमीतिलकचम्पकान्।
दाडिमी-पिप्पलीद्राक्षास्तथा कुसुममण्डपान्।। 23।।
जम्वीर-पूग-पनस-द्रुम-केतकीभि-
जाति-सरोज-शतपत्रिक-मल्लिकाभिः।
यन्नारिकेल-कदलीदलपाठालाभि-
युक्तें तदत्र भवनं श्रियमातनोति।। 24।।

पञ्चमोऽध्यायः

गृहप्रवेशविधिः

Unfortunately for us, the Sanskrit ślokas of the fifth chapter are too corrupted to be restored. B omits the whole chapter and C does not contain the Sanskrit ślokas, but only the Uriyā commentary. A contains the Sanskrit ślokas, in a corrupted form. It is a mystery how C lost the original Sanskrit ślokas and preserve only the Uriyā commentary. A has the following corrupted ślokas :

मेषसिंहं हयानान्तु पूर्वे शालः प्रशस्यते।
प्राडवुम् मुखं पश्चिमद्वारा प्रविश्यन्ते धनापते।। 1।।
वृषकन्यामृगानां च सप्तद्वाराणि मन्दिरे।
प्राङ्मुख उत्तरद्वारा दक्षिणभिमुख।। 2।।
तुलामिथुनकुम्भानां शुभेपश्चिममन्दिरे।
पूर्वाभिमुख पूर्वद्वारे सन्ति धनानि च।। 3।।
अलिकर्कटमीनानामुत्तरं मन्दिरं मतम्।
श्रीकामदक्षिणद्वारा प्रविश्यन्ति वरानन।। 4।।

It also contains a significant śloka, which ascribes the origin of the work of Viśvakarman :

नागस्थान स्थानद्वारे विश्वकर्मा च भाषित।
दोषगुण समासाद्य कथितं वास्तुविस्तरम्।।

C has the following in Uriyā on गृहप्रवेशविधि :

ब्राह्मणे सन्तुष्ट कराइ। वन्धु कुटुम्बे स्नेह वहि।। 51।।

मंगल उत्सव कराइ। गृहे प्रवेश हेव यांइ।। 52।।

श्रीमत भागवत थिव। सेठारे पठन होइव।। 53।।

जगनाथकुं सुमारिव। मणोहिं किछि कराइव।। 54।।

एरूपे ये नर करइ। केवेहें लक्ष्मी न छड़ाइ।। 55।।

विपत्तिमान पलाइवे। सुदर्शन रक्षा करिवे।। 56।।

नीलाद्रिपति पादे ध्यान। निरते रहु मोर मन।। 57।।

शिल्पलक्षण पदकेते। कहिलि एहा मुहिं गीते।। 58।।

सुजने मो दोष न धर। बाऊरी महाराणा छार।। 59।।

The above would thus be translated into English :

The ceremony of entering the new house would be held after satisfying the Brāhmins and getting the affection of friends and relatives and performing the auspicious festival. In the house there would be Śrīmadbhāgavata, which would be read on the occasion. One should remember the god Jagannātha (of Puri) and promise some present to the god. One, who observes the ceremony in this way, is never fortaken by the goddess Lakṣmī. All sorts of dangers flee away from him and the Sudarśana cakra would protect him. I pray that my mind would always remain attached to the feet of the Lord of Nīladrī. I have thus spoken of śilpalakṣaṇa in verses. I hope that the good people wood not look for my defects, because Bāurī Mahārana is a very humble man.

Again, *Silpi-laksana* is thus described in Uriya :

शिल्पिलक्षणकु येवे विचारिव।

विसिक्रमा मेरुकु कहुँ अछन्ति।।

हे मेरु शुन।

आचारवन्त होइव। शुचिवन्त होइव।।

तिरि पुंस घेनि थेव।

पुरुष वछा धरि थेव।।

एमन्त होइ शुभ पूजा कराइव।

ब्राह्मणवरण, विसिक्रमा वरण।।

नवग्रहवरण। एतेक वरण करिव।

एतेक वरण कले अश्वमेधधर्म होइ।।

हीन आचार्यकु न डाकिव।

हीन शिल्पि विन्धानिकि न डाकिव, विफलनिन्दा होइ।

से कीर्त्ति नपुंसक कीर्त्ति होइ।।

It may be translated thus :

Now, the Śilpi-lakṣaṇa should be discussed. Viśvakarman thus speaks to Meru : O, Meru, listen. The Yajamāna should be pure in habits. The auspicious work should be done along with his wife and children. Thus the pūjā should be done by invoking Brāhmaṇa, Viśvakarman, Navagraha. Thus one would get the result of Aśvamedha. Never call a bad ācārya or a bad śilpin, then your fame would be useless like an eunuch.

APPENDIX I

भूमिपरीक्षा, 1, s, 6.

cf. : Vāstu Vidyā, 2, 27-30 :

आज्यागन्धा च सा भूमिर्ब्राह्मणानां प्रशस्यते।
पूर्वप्लवा च रक्ता च कुशदर्भैरलङ्कृता।। 27।।
रक्तगन्धा च या भूमिः क्षत्रियाणां प्रशस्यते।
दक्षिणप्लवनोपेता कुशदर्भैरलङ्कृता।। 28।।
अन्नगन्धा च या भूमिः सा वैश्यानां प्रशस्यते।
पश्चिमप्लवनोपेता दूर्वाभिश्च समन्विता।। 29।।
सुरागन्धा च या भूमिः शूद्राणां समुदाहृता।
इन्द्रोन्नतं पुत्रनाशं वह्न्युन्नतमथार्थदम्।। 30।।

cf. : Mayamatam, 3, 5, 10 :

श्वेता रक्ता च पीता च कृष्णा कापोतसन्निभा।
तिक्ता च कटुका चैव कषायलवणाम्लका।। 5।।
**सा शुभा सर्ववर्णानां सर्वसम्पत्करी धरा।
दध्याज्यामधुरागन्धा च तैलासृग्गन्धिका च या।। 6।।

cf. : Agnipurāṇam, 92, 7 :

शुक्लाज्यगन्धा रक्ता च रक्तगन्धा सुगन्धिनी।
पीता कृष्णा सुरागन्धा विप्रादीनां मही क्रमात्।। 7।।

cf. : Matsyapurāṇam, 252, 11 13a :

पूर्वं भूमिं परीक्षेत पश्चाद्वास्तु प्रकल्पयेत्।
श्वेता रक्ता तथा पीता कृष्णा चैवानुपूर्वशः।। 21।।
विप्रादेः शस्यते भूमिरतः कार्यं परीक्षणम्।
विप्राणां मधुरास्वादा कटुका क्षत्रियस्य तु।। 22।।

तिक्ता कषाया च तथा वैश्यशूद्रेषु शस्यते।। 23।। क

cf. : मनुष्यालयचन्द्रिका, 2.29 :

श्वेता पाटलपीतमेचकरुचश्चाज्यासृगन्नासवा-

मोदाः स्वादुकषायतिक्तकटुकस्वादान्विताश्च स्मृताः।।

cf. : Śilparatna, 3. 24 :

श्वेता .... स्मृता।।

(Same as in the manuṣyalayācandrikā).

cf. : Bṛhatsamhitā, 53, 96 :

सितरक्तपीतकृष्णा विप्रादीनां प्रशस्यते भूमिः।

गन्धश्च भवति यस्या घृतरुधिरान्नाद्यमसमः।।

कुशयुक्ता शखहुत्वा दुर्वाकाशावृता क्रमेण मही।

अनुवर्णं वृद्धिकरी मधुरकषायाम्लकटुका च।।

cf. : वास्तुप्रकरणम् (Ms. in the Viśvabhāratī Library)

श्वेतवर्णे द्विजातीनां क्षत्रियाणां च लोहितं।। 60।।

पीतवर्णं तु वैश्यानां शूद्राणां कृष्णवर्णकं।

. . . मधुरं सर्ववर्णानां ब्राह्मणानां विशेषतः।। 61।।

क्षत्रियानां कषायं तु वैश्यानामाम्लमिष्यति।

शूद्राणां कटुतिक्तं च लक्षणं (?) परिवर्जयेत्।। 63।।

cf. : हयशीर्षपंचरात्रम् (पंचमः पटलः)

दधिक्षीराज्यगन्धा च मदिरासवगन्धिनी।

सुगन्धिव्रीहिगन्धा च शुभद्रव्य जला च या।। 67।।

cf. : हयशीर्षपंचरात्रम् (षष्ठः पटलः)

श्वेतारुणापीतकृष्णाविप्रादीनां प्रशस्यते।

आद्यासृगन्धा मद्यानां तुल्यगन्धातु या भवेत्।। 223।।

मधुरा च कषाया च अम्ला च कटुका च या।। 224क।।

भूपरीक्षा, 1, 8 :

cf. : Matsyapurāṇam, 253, 17-18 :

फालकृष्टेऽथवा देशे सर्वबीजानि वापयेत्।। 17।।

त्रिपंचसप्तरात्रे च यत्रारोहन्ति तान्यपि।

जेष्ठोत्तमा कणिष्ठा भूर्वर्जनीयतरा सदा।। 18।।

cf. : Mayamatam, 4, 4 :

कृष्ठा गोमयमिश्राणि सर्वबीजानि वापयेत्।

दृष्ट्वा तानि विरुढानि फलपक्वगतानि च।। 4।।

APPENDIX II

DESCRIPTION OF VĀSTU-PRAKARṆAṀ Ms.

The Ms. *Vāstuprakarṇaṁ* belongs to the Viśvabhāratī Library (No. 1614). It is written on paper in Davanāgarī character. There are 29 leaves. The condition of the Ms. is good. Neither the name of the copyist is given nor the date. There are eight lines to a page.

It begins time :

।। श्री गणेशाय नमः।। अथ वास्तु प्रकरणं।।
ब्रह्मशक्रयमश्चैव भगवांमिरसस्तथा।।
गौतमश्चैव गार्ग्यश्च मनुष्याश्चभृतस्तथा।। 1।।
विश्वकर्मादिभिश्चैव वास्तुविद्याविशारदैः।
सर्वेषां यत्कृतं शास्त्रं सारमुधृत्य यत्नतः।। 2।।

The Ms. ends abruptly at leaf 29. The Vāstuprakarṇam section ends at leaf 28 with the words :

।। इतिमंगलानि भवतु।। ।।श्री।। 7।।

WORDS-INDEX